When Bad Children Happen to Good Parents

"Survival Manual for Parents of Uncaring Children"

by
Norman E. Hoffman, Ph.D., Ed.D.

Revised Edition

♥
A Heart Book

When Bad Children Happen to Good Parents
A Survival Manual for Parents of Uncaring Children

A Heart Book

All rights reserved.
Copyright 1997 by Norman E. Hoffman
Cover Design copyright 1997 by Heart Publications No part of this book may be reproduced or transmitted in any form or by any means electronic or mechanical, including photocopying, recording, or by any information storage and retrieval system without permission in writing from the publisher.

PRINTED IN THE UNITED STATES OF AMERICA

**Library of Congress
Cataloging-in-Publication Data 96-095517**

Hoffman, Norman E.
　When Bad Children Happen to Good Parents
　by Norman E. Hoffman

ISBN 0-9652414-9-1

1. Uncaring Children Syndrome.
2. Child Psychology.
3. Parenting Skills.

Heart Books are published by
Heart Publications and Literary Agency.
It's trademark consisting of the words "Heart Books" and the portrayal of a ♥ is Registered in the U.S. Patent and Trademark Office.

Heart Publications and Literary Agency,
1186 Ocean Shore Blvd., Suite 167,
Ormond Beach, Florida 32176
(904) 441-6755

PREFACE

When Bad Children Happen to Good Parents: *A Survival Manual for Parents of Uncaring Children,* offers hope for parents who have been forced to accept guilt for the "antisocial" behavior of their children. It is a manual that challenges not only classical and modern psychology, but also the sacrosanct popular myth, "there are no bad children, only bad parents."

Readers will be introduced to the term *"Uncaring Child Syndrome,"* and the *"Uncaring Child,"* as it is used synonymously to characterize a child who lacks bonding and is generally disconnected from his/her caretakers. *Uncaring Children* lack a sense of guilt and remorse, blame others for their problems, misconduct, behaviors etc., and are skillful manipulators who demonstrate a fixed pattern of blatant hostility, selfishness, irresponsibility and callousness.

Many *Uncaring Children* are commonly diagnosed with Oppositional Defiant and Conduct Disorders. Although these diagnoses define some of the behavioral traits of children, the *Uncaring Child* also has some of the character traits of Antisocial Personality Disorder of adults. Therefore, diagnosing the *"Uncaring Child"* requires specific data to accurately differentially diagnose this condition.

Finally, there is someone who realizes that bad children "can" happen to good parents. And now there is help and hope for those parents seeking to correct the maladaptive behavior of their children.

Valerie G. Watt, Ph.D., LCSW

IN THE BEGINNING

The screams of the saber tooth and the wail of the triceratops were nightmarish tales told by the two frightened lovers. As they held each other tightly, bewildered and fearful, their dreams added to an already dreadful and unpleasant evening by the fire.

Confronted by their oldest sons' defiant and belligerent behavior, they felt they would never be able to curb his problematic conduct. This night, like many others, was filled with long hours of discussion between the couple. They were frustrated, angry and apprehensive of what was to become of their ungrateful and ungovernable son. His continued lying, stealing and disrespectful behavior made it impossible for them to feel comfortable, secure or positive when it came to their concerns for his future. What if their younger son would grow up to be like him? Could he be helped? The many lengthy discussions, their attempts to discipline him and their abundance of love failed to make any change.

They felt like failures in their rearing of Cain. They searched every element of their child's early development to uncover even the slightest hint of their failure as parents. They recalled how easily he got bored with play. They recalled his jealousy towards his younger brother when the newborn arrived; the fights over sharing his toys and fits of anger when he felt he was being treated unfairly.

They began to ask why their younger son, Abel, was such a model son. Adam was reminded by Eve how he would say, "Oh Eve, stop exaggerating. He's just going through a phase, he'll grow out of it." Adam stood up, seemingly annoyed, and walked pensively to the cave entrance. Eve followed and put her arms around him. Adam turned, now considering the question seriously. Well, if it's not a phase, what is it? We must have messed up somehow. It doesn't make sense. Ever since I can remember Abel has been such a good boy, so well behaved, such a gentleman. So what happened with his brother? He was born around the same time as Abel, in the same place, with all of the same opportunities and the same parents. But it seems to me, he doesn't seem to care much about anyone or anything. What went wrong?

Finally, Eve walked to where Cain was sleeping and began to weep. Adam joined her and gently nudged her to come back to sleep. Eve said, "There must be something we can do. I am worried something bad is about to happen. Cain shows no involvement or concern with the family. He never shows guilt for what he has done; he seems so jealous and envious of Abel. We had so many dreams of a healthy and happy family. What have we done? What can we do? Why does he behave like he does? I don't know what to do. One day Cain seems so loving - the next day - he's like someone I don't know. Someone without feeling or caring. The other day, I saw a look on Cain's face that frightened me. While Abel was planting flowers in the garden, Cain hit him with a rock. He then ran off with that damn pet snake of his, laughing. Although he said it was an accident, I know differently. It was no accident."

"Eve, that's ridiculous. In spite of his problem behavior, I can't believe he would ever intentionally hurt his brother."

"But Adam, there's something wrong with that boy, and there's been something wrong with him ever since I can remember."

TABLE OF CONTENTS

Preface i
In The Beginning iii

Chapter 1.
Am I Losing My Child — 1

Chapter 2.
Four Profiles of
The Uncaring Child Syndrome — 9

Chapter 3.
Anxiety: The Food for Change — 18

Chapter 4.
Early Signs of
the Uncaring Child Syndrome — 26

Chapter 5.
Follow The Leader — 50

Chapter 6.
Alcohol, Drugs and Crime — 65

Chapter 7.
The Treatment Process — 82

Chapter 8.
Ask The Doctor — 101

Conclusion 124
About The Author 125
References 129

1

Am I Losing My Child?

"Youth is disintergrating. The youngsters of the land have a disrespect for their elders, and a contempt for authority in every form. Vandalism is rife, and crime of all kinds is rampant among our young people. The nation is in peril."

Priest - Egypt, 2,000 BC

Not since the Vietnam War Experience have we seen such an alarming number of casualties. We are befuddled and feel totally helpless as we watch many of our children slip from us, our protection, our families. They seem uncaring, unloving and alien; they resist our pleas to stop destructive behavior that seem without goals and void of good judgment, remorse or any other feeling. Their defiance, selfishness, lack of learning from experience, superficiality, and broken promises increase; and our own hopes that they will "grow out of it" become unrealistic fantasies.

Am I Losing My Child?

By the time some of our children turn eight, we (the parents) can hardly believe their dramatic personality change and behavior that goes far beyond the boundaries of expected adolescent yearnings. We become conscious of their marked lack of guilt or remorse and their failure to deal with anything that may make them anxious.

Suddenly, we actually feel like we are at war. But who is the enemy? Is it the parents -- guilty of inadequate parenting? Do we not have the skills to understand and communicate with our children? Are we, as a society, so overwhelmed with stress that we are unable to meet the needs of our children?

As in any war, the pain and suffering is intense, and both sides suffer tremendously. Some of the most caustic wounds, most significant losses, are inflicted upon those whose lives the children touch. These children, themselves fulfilling a self-imposed prophecy of pain, are leaving a legacy of cost and sorrow to those around them. If we ignore the unquestionable fact that our kids could be in trouble in a troubled world, and if we fail to confront this tragic condition with a new set of rules and parenting skills, the loss of our children is imminent.

The trend in the United States has been to view children as basically good entities whose behavior is molded from a blueprint drawn by architects of the family, the parents.[1] When a child misbehaves, we look to the parents as culprits. Most writers and therapists place the blame, of 'children going bad' on the environment, or parents Jersild stated:

> This contrasts with some earlier speculations to the effect that criminal tendencies are inherited - the criminal springs from 'bad seed.' Actually, no delinquent has a gene - or a set of genes that produced in him a tendency to steal a horse or a car.[2]

Parents believe this because that's what they've been told, that they are not providing proper care and love, that they lack listening skills, that their actions have possibly damaged or retarded their child's normal development. Naturally, this belief causes guilt and self-recrimination in what may be an already disintegrated family. But often, regardless of how the parents try to remedy a problem, the child remains unresponsive and becomes even more of a problem.

Ginott[3] wrote of the costly consequences of an unhappy childhood. He stated, "We are deeply concerned lest we damage our children for life." He said, "She (talking about the mother of the child) would be more helpful if she had less guilt and more skill."

Samenow[4] suggested that there are kids who, no matter what the parents do, will "inflict enormous damage upon society." Initially, Samenow believed that criminal behavior was symptomatic of internal conflicts caused by early childhood trauma and deprivation. From his experience and research, he had to *unlearn* all that he had learned about the causation of criminal behavior; he now concludes that new methods are necessary to deal with these difficult children. His new approach is that criminals *choose* to commit crimes.[5]

It may be that these children's perception of the world is faulty. Studies have stated, "There is little doubt that bad people see the world differently from good."[6]

Sal

Sal, an eleven-year-old preadolescent boy, had been suspended three times for fighting and talking back to his sixth grade teacher. He lived with his mother, stepfather, and eight-year-old sister. Since first grade, teachers had indicated that Sal had difficulty keeping his mind on school work, disobeyed the rules, had frequent temper outbursts, was moody, and seemed to like playing the role of "class clown". After being called to school repeatedly because of Sal's misconduct, his parents sought the help of a family counselor. The expenses in time and money mounted as the family counselor advised them to "win Sal's cooperation" by planning family outings and involving Sal in weekly family meetings to discuss problems and relevant issues. The counselor suggested they try to be more reflective (a therapeutic skill introduced by psychologist Carl Rogers) in their listening skills and less authoritative, treating the boy with equality and using "I" messages. An I-message is a communication technique that helps share feelings and concerns in a non-threatening and nonjudgmental manner.[7] After several months, discouraged and beaten, the parents terminated treatment.

When I first became involved in the mental health profession in

1963, that advice was and continues to be, the standard intervention technique offered to most parents with similarly troubled children. Therapeutic literature is filled with the notion that a problem child is the fault of the parents. The implication is that the identified problem child is not the primary person responsible for the family's conflict -- a premise which is the hallmark of family counseling and focuses the blame on the parents. This concept unfortunately results from modern-day psychological belief that "there are no bad children, only bad parents," a teaching that singularly has caused needless guilt and delay in family progress or parenting process.[8]

Throughout the years parents, in their attempts to deal with problem children, have been left immobilized and powerless to cope with and improve family conflict, largely due to mental health professionals lacking understanding of the Uncaring Child Syndrome. Their attempts to help the family usually take the form of accusing good parents of being traumatizing and "bad," frustrating any possibility of their child's healthy development if changes are not made. Parents are left with undeserved guilt and self-reproach, making positive change impossible.

The belief that good parents can have bad children is generally unacceptable by the population at large. To suggest its possibility might also imply a complete breakdown in time-honored beliefs in the "sanctity" of children who theoretically are all born good and only become bad because of parental and environmental influences.

But what if there are children whose behavior is influenced primarily by their own selfish, single-minded needs to achieve pleasure and self-gratification, with little or no regard for others? These children would have no bonding with their parents or siblings; would blame others for their own failures and rarely, if ever, have insight into their behavior.

Such children do exist, and they see themselves as gentle and caring in their manipulative attempts to get involved with other human beings. Unfortunately, their tremendous inadequacy makes developing healthy and meaningful, lasting relationships impossible. What at first may look like close involvement and commitment is really the masquerade of an intimate relationship. For example, they may overly generalize philosophical statements which initially may be interpreted as wisdom but are later found to be a major barrier in communication. These same children may also indulge in excessive drinking, drug use, gambling, manipulation, sexual deviations and violence. These behaviors make them feel adequate and give them a sense of feeling fulfilled, at least temporarily. However, since they are unable to maintain a lasting and meaningful relationship, their self-esteem and identity becomes increasingly and constantly threatened.

The family is usually the most vulnerable target, and the most frequent contact for the Uncaring Child's manipulation because of his power and control over the ones who have the most to lose. "The one who has the most invested in a relationship has the least power."[9] In spite of emotional and physical pain the child inflicts on the parents, they continue to invest, time and time again, emotionally and physically in their child, their baby. To bear this horrid pain, the parents look to the past for answers and relief. They see their youngster as the cuddly, cute, adorable child who smiled, cooed, and positively justified their child rearing. They still see this youngster as a small child, growing, developing, and fulfilling their own dreams and fantasies of a normal, healthy, loving family. They then make excuses for their child's behavior and overlook significant cues and opportunities to intervene. These memories, the tendency to be blinded when it comes to seeing the child as "bad", and the monumental guilt and self reproach prolong and feed the flame of the child's unhealthy behaviors. Parents desperately want to believe and forgive; they make new agreements to gain their child's approval.

Unfortunately, they are again and again left frustrated, exasperated, and hopeless with their child's repeated performance of broken promises, lying, stealing and disobeying family rules.

As long as the child holds a power position in the family system, the youngster maintains control over the atmosphere, direction, goals and plans of the family. As the family continues to invest in hopes to connect with their child, the child's disconnection prevails and brings the family powerlessly to its knees. Parents are reduced to pleading for their child to understand their feelings, and they attempt to instill a sense of guilt so the youngster will appreciate their pain. Instead, the child avoids them and blames them for the prevailing dilemma, demanding further freedom while attempting to be portrayed as a victim of constrictive and uncaring parents. These children are masters of fixing the blame on parents, siblings, teachers and peers. Skillful manipulators, these children can interweave half-truths into a rational and believable story, thereby becoming vindicated from any wrong-doing in their own mind.

Penelope Leach, author of Children First, stated: "Parents are the victims of monumental social injustice." "They are having a lousy time, and it isn't their fault."[10] She puts the blame for the parents' impotency on society, government and business policies that don't support parents' needs.

For the purpose of this book, and since *antisocial, sociopathic,* and *psychopathic* have virtually the same meaning, the term *antisocial* will be used exclusively to describe certain acts. A distinction must be made between antisocial behavior and antisocial *criminal* behavior. The antisocial behavior of the Uncaring Child is not socially acceptable, but the child may not necessarily become a criminal. For example, an individual who lies, skips school and is disrespectful may be antisocial, but he is not a criminal. While an antisocial act is always involved when a crime is committed, a crime is not always involved when an antisocial act is committed. It is this distinction that separates the antisocial from the antisocial criminal.

Antisocial Characteristics

Antisocial behaviors are those ascribed to people who demonstrate a fixed pattern of blatant hostility, selfishness, irresponsibility and callousness. They have great difficulty forming significant loyalties to individuals or groups. They behave in ways that often result in legal or social offenses. Unable to learn from experience, such people are resistant to all forms of psychotherapeutic intervention. Cleckley[11] listed the following characteristics of antisocial behavior:

1. Superficial charm and intelligence

2. Absence of delusions and other signs of irrational thinking

3. Absence of nervousness or psychoneurotic manifestations

4. Unreliability
5. Untruthfulness
6. Lack of remorse or shame
7. Inadequately motivated antisocial behaviors
8. Poor judgment and failure to learn by experience
9. Pathologic egocentricity in the capacity for love
10. General poverty in major affective reactions
11. Specific loss of insight
12. Unresponsiveness in general interpersonal relationships
13. Fantastic and uninviting behavior with drinking and sometimes without
14. Suicide rarely carried out
15. Sex life, impersonal, trivial and poorly integrated
16. Failure to follow any life plan

The psychodynamic interpretation that follows was the hallmark of my earlier thinking when forming a theory to account for antisocial behavior: Until 1982, I accepted the psychoanalytic theory, holding analytic interpretation sacred. But when I began working with the families of Uncaring Children in South Florida, I found it difficult to continue in such rigid, narrow view. I began to treat children whose siblings had no unusual problems with their families, school, or interpersonal relationships.

According to psychoanalytic theory,[12] antisocial personality has its roots during the first fifteen months of development. These children are frustrated and confused and may experience massive rejection by their parents. Upon reaching puberty and during adolescence, these children may suffer from excessive frustration and anxiety caused by this rejection. This makes it almost impossible for them to form healthy relationships. Very clearly these children have been massively and continuously traumatized throughout their childhood, and they have had difficulties identifying with a healthy parent. These early unresolved conflicts cause severe structural defects in their personality.

Until 1982, I believed that for antisocial behavior to exist, there must be unhealthy developmental factors in the form of parental deviance, rejection, or separation. Also, that there could not be meaningful and healthy relationship in early development. But I was bothered by one thing. How could parents raise two or three seemingly healthy children, and only one become antisocial? What was I missing? Must I dig deeper into early development? Were there family secrets that were being kept from me?

The greater question for me was, are we causing unnecessary hardships and monumental guilt for good parents with bad kids?

If the answer is yes, what characterizes the obvious behavior of the adolescents who refuse to cooperate and choose to continue in their maladaptive, disruptive and disturbing actions. Why is there such a disparity in the feelings and attitudes of the Uncaring Child? What are the early warning signs? How do they become uncaring? What do they feel? Can they be helped? Whose fault is it that they become this way?

This manual attempts to answer these questions and bring better understanding to parents struggling to raise moral, caring children. Evidence shows that an increasing number of children, who do not necessarily fit into the diagnostic category of antisocial personality and who do not commit criminal acts, engage in behaviors destructive to themselves and others. Therefore, they do not successfully participate in interpersonal and social relationships.[13] It is these children who fit the profile of the Uncaring Child.

2

Four Profiles of The Uncaring Child Syndrome

"Youth is a malady of which one becomes cured a little every day."

Benito Musolini - 15th Birthday

THE CHAMELEON:

Carrie

Thirteen-year-old Carrie was brought to me by her parents who complained that she lied, ran away from home, and was argumentative. Her grades in school were dropping because she was not doing her homework.

When Carrie was six years old, her parents had been concerned about their daughter's lack of self-motivation in her play. At the same time she seemed to become easily bored. In spite of her parent's many attempts to motivate and interest her in various projects, Carrie's pattern was usually the same. When something new was presented, she at first became excited and enthusiastic,

Four Profiles of the Uncaring Child Syndrome

only to lose interest after a few minutes. There was one notable exception; when Carrie's playmates showed interest in the same thing, her enthusiasm and interest continued. Apparently Carrie's behavior was energized only by copying others; but at the same time she was unable to crystallize and maintain her own identity. She acted as if she had thought of the ideas and projects herself, when in fact, they came from others.

While her parents spent a lot of time "entertaining" her in efforts to motivate self-interest, they also reported their fear that she "never" felt remorse or guilt for any of her actions that caused pain to others. She could not be counted on to complete chores, projects, or any other commitment she would agree to, in spite of continued talks about responsibility and threats of punishment.

Carrie displayed another important warning sign by refusing to deal with any unpleasant problems she may have caused. No matter how often her parents pressed her to discuss and resolve any such conflict, Carrie's usual response was, "I've already dealt with it. It's in the past. Why don't you ever stop talking about the same things?" She lacked empathy, genuineness, and sincere warmth in any relationship that demanded more than a superficial understanding.

Further exploration revealed a girl who had no attachments to her personal belongings. In fact, she gave away, lost or misused her personal belongings, regardless of her parents' attempts to get her to appreciate them. This lack of regard for her belongings carried over to a blatant lack of concern for other people's property. She would borrow, then lose or misuse her friends' and parents' items with equal disregard.

When Carrie was eight years old, her parents began to hear from her playmates, bizarre tales that Carrie was unloved, abused, and unwanted by her parents. These lurid lies brought total frustration and tears to loving, caring parents whose daughter was the most cherished person in their lives.

Summarizing Carrie's profile, we see a child with the budding traits of the Uncaring Child Syndrome - a child who presented a *chameleon* like facade with no inner substance. She seemed to resent and repel all expressions of concern from those who loved her, defying the empathetic understanding and regard that is so necessary for a healthy and meaningful relationships to exist. No sense of bonding or connection ever existed between her and her parents or between her and her friends. Ironically, Carrie believed she was a loving and caring child with many "close and loyal friends." Her reality seemed distorted; she was unable or unwilling to appreciate what others were attempting to elicit from her or make her feel. She could not - or would not - understand their pain or allow herself to be seen as the one who created it.

Jonathan

Jonathan was fourteen when his parents requested my help. They came to me anxious and fearful that their son would run away and possibly become involved in the drug scene. They explained that he was unwilling to do homework, his grades were failing, and he was "hanging around" with peers his parents described as undesirable. At home he watched TV excessively, avoided involvement in family activities, disregarded daily chores, and generally lacked interest or motivation in almost all daily functions.

Jonathan's parents told me that throughout his life, he had lacked self-motivation and interest. Whenever his friends expressed any interest whatsoever, Jonathan acted as if he generated that interest himself. For instance, when Jonathan expressed an interest in a specific jazz artist, he would enthusiastically discuss the artist and his music. He would purchase many of the artist's recordings and play them to his parents. He seemed to take great delight in demonstrating his interest to his parents, who also expressed happiness in his newly found enthusiasm. But they soon discovered that Jonathan's interest was, in fact, the interest of his friend. When his friend's interest waned, so did Jonathan's.

The *chameleon* is like a lizard capable of changing his color. He is also able to change his disposition or habits. This individual's whole relation to life lacks genuineness. The chameleon does not see anything wrong with himself, and he is devoid of any traces of warmth. He gives the impression of a making good adjustment to life, but he actually takes on the personalities of others and copies their ideas and ideals. He is ready to adopt any and all of their attitudes. reactions and behaviors that he feels are expected. Thus, he has no real, identifiable personality. He appears to shift from thing to thing and person to person.

THE OPERATOR:

Operators are charming, ingratiating, and an expert at wheeling, dealing, and conning parents and others. Operators display a high degree of dominance and are thought to be well liked by their peers. However, they rarely learn from mistakes and relentlessly engage in deceptions, without concern for others, for momentary gain.

Lenny

Lenny was a successful twenty-five-year-old patient expounding on some of his earlier achievements. He boasted of how he was able to sell poor people used pianos and organs, promising a 100% guarantee. He bragged about never making good on any complaints, maneuvering his corporation to avoid any possible litigation. A failing marriage and difficulty with his children finally brought him into counseling. During the entire therapy process, Lenny maintained an impenetrable barrier making any intervention impossible. He was convinced he was right and everyone else was wrong. His superficial charm, yet lack of insight, made all attempts to change his behavior frustrating. The result of his unbending attitude was the disillusionment of his marriage and divorce.

Manny

While treating Manny and Marlene for marital problems, I learned that Manny, a thirty-year-old insurance agent, had cheated and lied to some of his clients. Although he attempted to present himself as a man of integrity, his wife portrayed him as someone who would con, lie and steal from anyone. Some positive changes were seen early in therapy; however, Manny returned to his previous antisocial behavior once therapy ended. Several additional attempts at marital counseling were uneventful. Manny was a great con man. He had all the charm and "gift of gab" necessary for his trade. Unfortunately, he had little regard for the rights of others. He felt no shame, guilt or remorse for his uncaring actions.

Sharon

Sharon was sixteen years old when her parents contacted me. She had been suspended from school because she falsified absences. Sharon would write fraudulent excuses, supposedly signed by her parents, in order to cut school. She carried this off for almost six months without being found out and she developed a network of peers to assist her in her elaborate scheme to skip classes. Sharon also had been researching the drug market and asking a lot of questions about the sale of drugs. Her school counselor spoke to some of her peers corroborating this fact. Sharon was considering becoming a drug dealer, repackaging over-the-counter caffeine pills and selling them as quality "speed." Although she had not committed any criminal act to that point, she appeared likely to become involved in antisocial criminal acts.

Sharon's parents told me that as a child, she liked to be the "boss." She seemed to have many friends, but *she* was always the leader. Whenever Sharon was caught doing something wrong, she seemed able to maneuver herself out of the problem. "She had answers for everything." Sharon's parents told me of her unique ability to change the circumstance of conflict or even her original statements, to make her appear guiltless. Sharon rarely, if ever, felt bad when her behavior created havoc for her family. Her lying, stealing, and false promises left her family with tremendous emotional pain.

Investigating early behavioral tendencies of all these individuals, I began to see a set of predominate patterns. All of the parents recalled their children's preoccupation with their own pleasures, problems, and self-gratification. Some of these kids felt rejected in spite of their family's attempts to develop togetherness. A feeling of bonding and a sense of intimacy with parents seldom occurred due to their indifference.

THE HELLBENDER:

The *hellbender* is the child who behaves a little more daringly than his peers. He appears to take unnecessary risks and is accident prone. He is the proverbial accident waiting to happen.

Four Profiles of the Uncaring Child Syndrome

Valerie

Valerie was fifteen years old when I initially saw her. She had been suspended from school for rather harmless pranks. When confronted with her behavior, She stated confidently that her teacher had "overreacted" to things that were "minor and incidental." She could not understand why the teacher "got on my case." However, Valerie's pranks, although minor were disruptive behavior that continued in spite of repeated attempts by her teacher to curtail. Valerie's similar and repeated problems in other classes prompted the principal to suspend her.

Her parents told me that she was always a child who "went past the point of no return." When she was five, she climbed on furniture to get to the kitchen cabinets. In spite of falling on several occasions, this behavior persisted. Throughout her entire childhood she would place herself in danger regardless of her parents' many warnings. During play she would run about without regard for the safety of others or herself. She would climb the monkey bars higher and swing higher than her peers, and she delighted in exploring areas of the playground that were off limits to children.

Barry

Seventeen-year-old Barry was referred to me by his parents after he had been arrested for driving while intoxicated. They described him as having repeated disciplinary difficulties with school authorities, being truant and failing at school. He was incorrigible. He fought with his peers and encountered police because of reckless driving.

He described his parents as being overly controlling, demanding and generally making his life a "living hell." He blamed his teachers for "picking" on him and claimed the police harassed him. He threatened to leave home so he would no longer be a bother to anyone.

Barry's parents portrayed him as a "boy with vengeance." They said that he had always created turmoil at home and in the neighborhood when he was growing up. While playing in the house, he would play catch with any object available, regardless of how fragile. He had broken the dining room chandelier by swinging on it after seeing a Tarzan movie. He would place objects in the electrical sockets to see what would happen. His fascination with matches once caused him to accidentally set the garage on fire. In spite of his parents' repeated attempts to change his behavior, Barry continued his reckless pursuit.

Uncaring and even antisocial individuals occupy some of the highest offices in the government of the United States. How often do we read or hear about prominent figures accused and sometimes convicted of cold and shameless crimes unbefitting and incongruent to what we expected from them.

THE TRANSFORMER:

The *transformer* is the child who, in the beginning, for all intents and purposes was the "good child." When parents discuss this child, they say, "He was such a good child." "She did what she was told the first time." "He never gave me any trouble." But at the age of about twelve, he becomes a markedly different individual, now uncaring and disobedient. The parents cannot understand what has happened to their loving offspring, the cause of this condition or what to do to change it.

Peter

Peter, at fifteen, came to me because he was disobedient, refused to do homework, failed in school and verbally assaulted his mother. He also was in love with a seventeen-year-old girl who was a high school dropout. He wanted to drop out of school when he turned sixteen, go to work as a laborer, leave his parents' home and live with his girlfriend.

Peter's parents characterized his childhood as uneventful. They said his early development had been normal; in fact, he had been the "perfect child." An average student, he had no unusual problems throughout school. But when he reached the age of twelve, his parents noticed a shift from being "good" to being "bad." He began to lie about his homework. He cut up in class to the point of being branded the "class clown," and became disobedient.

His parents also made me aware of another peculiar behavior. He began to malign his mother, displaying anger and contempt for having been unfairly and poorly treated. Whenever he perceived he was being denied, he would slander her and become depressed and angry. Whatever went wrong with him at school or at home was blamed on his mother. He got a certain feeling of relief when his disruptive behavior was discovered, appearing to derive a disturbing pleasure from being found out and punished.

Although the parents reported nothing unusual about his childhood development, further exploration of his personality traits revealed some interesting facts. As a child, although he had few friends, Peter had been unable to sustain interest in self-motivated play. In other words, he became bored easily when playing by himself. He seemed to do best when playing with other children.

I also learned that Peter was a follower. He would almost always join in the activities of others and follow their lead. He rarely challenged his peers, and when he did, he soon disengaged by submitting to others. When Peter reached the age of twelve, he began challenging his mother's position of authority with caustic and demeaning remarks. His behavior progressively worsened by the time he was fifteen. It should be noted he rarely challenged his father.

Peter's girlfriend came into the picture when he turned fifteen. She was characterized as a very strong and dominant individual from a lower social and economical class. At first she was described as a "sweet young girl," well liked by Peter's parents. After a short time, when Peter's behavior became more assaultive and argumentative, his parents felt he was in "her control" and no longer willing to work out their differences.

Much like the *chameleon*, Peter appeared to take on his girlfriend's characteristics and mannerisms, and his role became strengthened and reinforced by her positive acknowledgments. Being unaware of his personality transformation, he focused his energy more on his "bad mother," who he saw as overly controlling and guilt producing.

Susan

Susan, much like Peter, was described as the "perfect child."

When she was about thirteen, her parents began to notice changes in her behavior. She lied about her whereabouts and homework. By the time she was fourteen, she was coming home late from school and from her girlfriend's house. Her lying got progressively worse, and she became more negative and belligerent with authority figures.

Susan's involvement with her peers seemed to have a profound effect on her transformation. She, too, was described as a child who usually followed the lead of others. When she became involved with older peers, she took on some of their traits and portrayed herself as "bad."

If Susan's parents had been more skilled in recognizing the early signs of the *transformer*, they may have been more effective in mediating and resolving the problem at its onset. Unfortunately, most parents are told by their pediatricians, school counselors, and therapists that "This is just a phase of development, and it will soon pass."

3

Anxiety: The Food For Change

Someone once said, "Boys will be boys."
He forgot to add, "Boys will be men."

When I began working with the children at the Devereux Foundation in Devon, Pennsylvania, in 1963, the kids impressed me with not only their broad spectrum of emotional disturbance, but also a degree in which they experienced hurt, rejection and anxiety.

For example, Joe, a sixteen-year-old male, was depressed over the divorce of his parents, the subsequent absence of his father and the rejection of his mother. His mood was sullen and he remained withdrawn from our staff and his peers. Initial attempts to form a relationship with him were met with further withdrawal and a frozen posture. Any confrontation by his peers resulted in heightened anxiety and deepened depression (his face would become flush and his voice tremulous) as tears streamed down his cheeks.

The anxiety caused by such emotional pain is unwanted, but this subjective anxiety can be treated most successfully because of the nature of its pain. Subjective anxiety stems from the individual's awareness of his depression, his perceived role in its cause, the resultant guilt, and the fear of continued emptiness that seems unavoidable.[14]

> Anxiety is one of the central concepts of interpersonal psychiatry. Sullivan employs this term in a special way. By anxiety he means virtually all basic types of emotional suffering. This anxiety includes anxiousness, eerie loathing, guilt, shame, dread, feelings of personal worthlessness and other less definable painful feelings. Anxiety varies in degree from mild discomfort that is scarcely noticeable to disorganizing, incapacitating panic.

As Sullivan emphasized,

> ... the basic cause of anxiety is a strong threat to the emotional balance and well-being of the individual - that is, a threat to his integrity as a person. Such a threat is the result of emotional turmoil, both inside the person and in his relationships with people; this turmoil is caused by traumatic interpersonal relationships in both past and present life situations. As the individual senses that his emotional stability is being menaced, or even crumbling, he is flooded by the profound feeling of dread and apprehension we call anxiety.[15]

The symptoms associated with subjective anxiety include increased heart activity, sweating, disturbed breathing, dizziness, apprehension, and feelings of impending doom. Obviously, this picture is that anyone would want removed. Subjective anxiety is unwanted, frightening, and persistent, creating pain and suffering for those afflicted.

Another cause of depression and subjective anxiety is in the notion of hidden guilt. Some children emerge from their childhood with profound inner turmoil caused by a traumatic event or by an unhealthy relationship that led to the formation of overwhelming guilt. The child experiences symptoms of anxiety but has no idea what may be the cause. He/she may evidence heart palpitations, cold sweaty palms, hyperventilation, tremulous hands, facial muscular tension, and feelings of imminent death. But these obvious signs of inner turmoil and outward severe distress are actually what make a more positive treatment possible.

The adolescent who is reprimanded by his/her teacher for misbehaving may experience insecurity, rejection and distress from his perceived threat, or anger and dislike for the perceived advisory. In any case, the adolescent may become uneasy and discomforted by his newly shaken security and the unknown consequences of his actions. It is within this new framework that the anxiety flourishes.

Another cause of anxiety should be obvious in the following example: A fourteen-year-old girl was grounded by her parents for not doing her homework, lying, and making poor grades. The girl's first response was anger and withdrawal from her family. But because of some understanding but firm parental intervention, she began to express remorse and humiliation for doing so poorly, and she acknowledged the reality of her responsibility. She expressed fear of loss of her parents' love. Her manifest anger and withdrawal was a defense against experiencing further rejection and guilt. When her parents talked to her about their love for her and demonstrated they would not accept her misbehavior, the fourteen-year-old's manifest guilt, anxiety, and fear of loss, emerged.

A child who fails to experience subjective anxiety will rarely understand or appreciate family pain and the need for cooperation and change. This child feels only the pain of the moment, which lasts only as long as the conflict is paramount. As soon as the pressure is diminished, they resume their pattern of irresponsibility and indifference.

Contrary to subjective anxiety and its positive prognosis for treatment, the Uncaring adolescent experiences another kind of anxiety - objective anxiety. The Uncaring person indeed experiences anxiety, but it is the anxiety of the moment and it lasts as long as the perceived threat is present. They may be awaiting a hearing for a legal infraction, wondering if they will be found out for lying to their parents or they may be merely hiding their failing grades. But this objective anxiety subsides as soon as the threat is gone. If anxiety lasts only for the moment, and the person is able to escape uncomfortable situations without regard or remorse for those who they have hurt, one can quickly understand the difficulty in helping this individual to work on mediating and resolving interpersonal conflicts.

When we think about behavioral or emotional problems of children, we become concerned with a multitude of issues. Are these children being properly cared for by their parents? Are they suffering emotional, physical, or sexual abuse? Are they depressed or anxious? However, how often do we consider the widespread emotional and physical abuse that children can perpetrate on their parents? To understand the immense suffering of the family, we must first recognize parents' and family members' attempts to help the Uncaring Child, in spite of continued rejection, alienation, and abuse by the child. This can be better understood by the following example:

John

Thirteen-year-old John was referred to me by the school counselor. John's parents reported an array of problematic behaviors that had begun in the first grade. His current problems included disobeying teachers, instigating fights, walking out of class, using profanity, refusing to obey family rules or to do chores, lacking concern for the rights of others and making poor grades. John's eleven-year-old brother was a good student who had no problems at home or school and easily formed and maintained interpersonal relationships.

John's parents worked in middle class jobs and adequately provided for all the children's emotional and material needs. Both parents themselves had come from healthy and caring parents with whom they maintained close relationships. There was nothing noteworthy in either parents' past that would suggest family pathology. Both parents entered into marriage with the hopes of raising healthy children and providing them with all of the love and guidance they could give. Neither was ready or prepared for what was to occur. The parents reported nothing unusual during John's first six years. When he entered first grade, they began getting reports from the teacher of his stubbornness, oppositional behavior, and inattentiveness. This scenario continued throughout elementary

Anxiety: The Food For Change

school. He was suspended four times for fighting, being disobedient, and cursing. His parents said that John had lied, was untrustworthy, and aggressive. He stole money from them, broke the rules at home, and had temper outbursts, throwing or breaking things when angry.

After repeated attempts to change John's maladaptive behavior, his parents engaged a mental health professional to counsel John and the family. The counselor insisted that the parents needed to be less restrictive and allow their child to express himself more freely. He also encouraged reflective listening techniques and "I" messages so they might win his cooperation. After three months of therapy, the family dropped out of treatment because they saw no meaningful change in behavior.

Two more attempts at therapy were also unsuccessful. John's parents were contacted regularly by school personnel about his repeated problematic behavior. John's mother had to make excuses to her boss so she could leave work to deal with her son's problems at school.

As the problem continued without resolve, a rift between the parents began to widen due to the perceived softening or hardening of discipline by either parent. As John's behavior became the predominant focus of daily attention, the atmosphere in the home became cold, anxiety-ridden, and unfriendly. His brother became more isolated and absent in family matters. Additional pain was felt by the maternal grandparents due to John's rude and uncaring attitude when they came for a visit during a two-week vacation.

The family was in severe conflict and experiencing significant pain, loss, frustration and disillusionment. John's uncaring and indifferent attitude toward their despair further aggravated an already miserable and decaying situation. But they continued to make every effort to reach him and make him feel their pain.

Unfortunately, their attempts were in vain. In fact, their repeated and fruitless attempts not only caused further turmoil and despair, but reinforced their powerlessness to an already power-mad John. He remained fully in charge of the emotional health of the family. In spite of John's continued alienation from the family, they repeatedly but futilely expended emotional and physical energy to get him to behave in a caring and unselfish manner.

To understand the nature and extent of this horrifying problem, we must recognize the conditions that apparently foster and nurture its existence and perpetuation. To illustrate this, lets look at the case of one thirteen-year-old female patient who did not arrive home from school at her scheduled time. Her frantic parents spent the next two hours calling the school, neighbors, and her friends. Finally, they received a phone call from their baby-sitter, who was several miles from their home, informing them that their daughter was with her. The child told them she had been held down by several boys on the bus and was prevented from exiting. But her friends revealed that the child had been playing and cutting up with her girlfriends and several boys, causing her to miss her stop. Upon confrontation, she denied what her friends had reported and began to make further accusations about their character. It wasn't until the child was confronted by her "best friend" and her parents that she broke down and admitted her action. However, she accused her parents, friends and schoolmates of "hating" her. She held fast to a tale of never being loved or cared for.

This illustration describes two major defense mechanisms at work. First, the child *denied* any wrongdoing or responsibility for her actions, and then *projected* the blame on others when denial was unsuccessful. These defenses are usually present when the Uncaring Child is faced with anxiety producing situations. Because anxiety is painful and unwanted, the Uncaring Child will, at any cost, maintain and nurture any position necessary to avoid it, even at the expense and emotional cost to her family.

June

June was a seventeen-year-old who her father described as a "pathological liar." Other than detecting her lying behavior, her parents had always seen her as warm and loving. However, they are now questioning whether she really cared at all. They had lost their trust in anything June said. They also experienced a loss in their ability to love her as they had in the past.

June revealed a significant piece of information that has become the cornerstone in assessing similar individuals. The following dialogue will illustrate:

Anxiety: The Food For Change

Therapist: *"Why did you feel you had to falsify your teacher's signatures on your progress report?"*

June: *"I didn't want to get punished."*

Therapist: *"Punished?"*

June: *"Yeah! You see, my mom and dad would yell and never let up."*

Therapist: *"So you forged the signatures not to get yelled at?"*

June: *"Yeah?"*

Therapist: *"Do you recall the last family session, when your parents reminded you that they never yell or punish you when you tell the truth, and you agreed?"*

June: *"Well... I guess so."*

Therapist: *"When you learned your father contacted the school about your progress report, what did you feel? Were you frightened about being found out?"*

June: *"Not really. You see, I knew I could talk my way out of it when I got home. So, I really wasn't worried."*

Therapist: *"I understand you discovered your father contacted the school in the morning. Was there any fear at all during the rest of the school day?"*

June: *"No. Why should I be afraid? I knew I could get out of it. It was completely out of my mind. When I got home, I was a little nervous, but that didn't get in the way of talking to my dad."*

Therapist: *"So you continued to lie in spite of knowing your parents were informed of the truth?"*

June: *"Yeah! That may sound dumb, but I've done it before -- and got away with it."*

This dialogue is typical of children like June. Not only do they show disregard for values and principles, but they do not experience the *anxiety* that would be normally expected. The following sessions with June were uneventful. She continued to view therapy as a "waste of time" while attempting to diminish her wrongdoing. Therapy was then directed to working with her parents. The task was to diminish the parents' anxiety and attempt to place the anxiety onto June. Without June experiencing anxiety, positive change could not be expected. When children are resistive to working through the problems they cause, I find it more useful to direct my attention to the parents. When we give them the tools to facilitate change in their children, we may have a more positive outcome for their children.

Dealing with June's lack of concern or anxiety was the focus of therapeutic attention. After proposing a plan to make June responsible for her actions and consequences, initial progress was noted. Progress was interrupted by June running of with her boyfriend. Her parents continued to feel guilt and emotional pain because of their perceived failure. They blamed themselves for not being able to resolve June's problems earlier.

June was neither bothered by nor able to identify with anxiety in spite of her parent's confrontation. It is this missing link, the lack of anxiety, that *must* be present before any meaningful behavioral changes can be made. Working on changing misbehavior should be started as early as noticed. If June's parents had the knowledge of early signs and skills necessary when she was younger, there may have been a more positive outcome.

4

Early Signs of The Uncaring Child Syndrome

> *"Sometimes when I look at my children I say to myself, "Lillian, you should have stayed a virgin."*
>
> Mrs. Lillian Carter

Soft Signs

My early attempts to lay the groundwork for a concise manual on the Uncaring Child Syndrome (UCS) involved in lengthy and painstaking explorations into past and present literature dealing with antisocial and conduct disorders. Once I had a firm grasp on this body of accumulated knowledge, I began taking a closer look at the early developmental signs in the patients I was treating. Were there similarities in the early behavior that could be better understood? Were there test instruments I could use that would shed light on these behaviors? Was it possible to objectively describe a sufficient number of behaviors to spot this syndrome in its early stage and, hopefully, prevent it?

The following sources are detailed to give the reader a sampling of several pertinent references to the subject matter as well as the author's review and clinical criteria:

Behavioral Indicators of Delinquent Youngsters

Samenow[16] discusses behavioral indicators of delinquent youngsters, summarily listing them as follows:

1. Expecting others to indulge him or her
2. Voracious adventurous appetite
3. Risk taker
4. Embroiled in difficulties
5. Demanding
6. Projects blame on others
7. Denies wrongdoing
8. Dismisses usual recognition of good deeds
9. Seeks the forbidden
10. Temper tantrums
11. Irresponsible
12. Manipulative
13. Knack for forgetfulness
14. Defiant
15. Poor response to assist with family chores
16. Contempt for advice

Diagnostic Criteria For Antisocial Personality

The Diagnostic and Statistical Manual (DSM-IV)[17] formulates the diagnostic criteria for the Antisocial Personality Disorder. The following is taken from that source:

Early Signs of The Uncaring Child Syndrome

A. There is a pervasive pattern of disregard for and violation of the rights of others occurring since age 15 years, as indicated by three (or more) of the following:

    (1) failure to conform to norms with respect to lawful behaviors as indicated by repeatedly performing acts that are grounds for arrest,

    (2) deceitfulness, as indicted by repeated lying, use of aliases, or conning others for personal profit or pleasure,

    (3) impulsivity or a failure to plan ahead,

    (4) irritability and aggressiveness, as indicated by repeated physical fights or assaults,

    (5) reckless disregard for safety of self or others,

    (6) consistent irresponsibility, as indicated by repeated failure to sustain consistent work behavior or honor financial obligations, and

    (7) lack of remorse, as indicated by being indifferent to or rationalizing having hurt, mistreated, or stolen from another.

B. The individual is at least age 18 years.

C. There is evidence of Conduct Disorder (see p. 94) with onset before age 15 years.

D. The occurrence of antisocial behavior is not exclusively during the course of Schizophrenia or a Manic episode.

Conduct Disorder

The American Psychiatric Association[18] stated, "The essential feature of conduct disorder is a repetitive and persistent pattern of behavior in which the basic rights of others or major age-appropriate societal norms or rules are violated." Much controversy exists regarding the lack of distinction between antisocial and conduct behavior. Much of the Conduct Disorder behavior listed in DSM-IV is similar to *Uncaring Behavior*.

The major distinction between Conduct Disorder and *Uncaring Behavior* is *uncaring* children have a history of *Uncaring Behavior* during early childhood. They lack guilt, remorse and anxiety when it would be expected and appropriate.

The preceding list of behavioral and attitudinal indicators provides us with a realistic understanding that helps reduce or remove parents' guilt and anxiety. Parents also feel support in knowing that there are many "good parents" whose children's behavior is *not* a product of bad parenting. They realize that often good parents have children who show the described behaviors. This list, however, only supports the evidence that many similarities in unhealthy behavioral patterns exist in children regardless of their being raised by "good" or "bad" parents. I was still searching for a more comprehensive understanding of early warning signs that could help parents make strategic and early interventions. My first task was to review all my files of children with Conduct Disorders. I then gathered the information of those adolescents that matched Cleckley's[19] clinical picture of Antisocial Personality.

Common Problem Behaviors

A review of the literature assisted in my quest for understanding and identifying early warning signs. Turecki[20] categorized common types of problem behavior and parents' descriptions. The list is as follows:

Types of Behaviors	Parents' Descriptions
Defiant:	-Does whatever he wants -Ignores what I say -Does exactly the opposite of what I tell him

Early Signs of The Uncaring Child Syndrome

Resistive:	-Refuses to listen -Won't follow directions -Dawdles -Always finds excuses

Inattentive:	-Doesn't "listen" -Tunes out -Daydreams

Stubborn:	-Has to get his own way -Won't take no for an answer

Shy:	-Very timid -Clings to my skirts -Always hides his or her face

Particular:	-Very picky -Faddy -Only wants certain things -Really hard to please -Fussy, always noticing little

Complaining:	-Whines a lot -Pouts -Sulks -Never satisfied

Continued on Next Page

Interrupting:	-Breaks into adult conversations -Won't let me talk on the phone
Intrusive:	-Swears a lot -Calls people names, even adults
Selfish:	-Takes toys from other children -Rude -Won't share toys with siblings or friends -Everything is "mine"
Wild Behavior:	-Gets overexcited -Gets revved up easily -Creates a disturbance -Can be destructive
Impulsive:	-Loses control -Has outbursts over small things -Can't seem to stop
Physically Aggressive:	-Pushes and shoves people -Hits, kicks, or bites other children or even adults

Continued on Next Page

Temper Tantrums:	-May vary in intensity and duration

Weisberg and Greenberg[21] referred to the problem child as having a disruptive disorder. In their experience, disruptive children are most often discovered by age seven. "Disruptive classroom behavior at this age makes it increasingly evident that something is wrong."[22]

The literature reveals an increase in the number of problem children. Fortunately, a few authors are beginning to recognize the existence of behavior not explained by bad parenting.

I felt that this study was a beginning in determining early warning signs of the Uncaring Child Syndrome (UCS). I then compiled data from parents whose children had serious behavioral disorders, as well as utilizing test material[23] and began to inquire in more detail the early developmental stages of my patients evidencing this syndrome. What follows is a list of those attitudes and behaviors most commonly found from my review of children evidencing the UCS -- children ranging four to nineteen years old. The *uncaring child* may have a few to several of the following behaviors:

Attitudes & Behaviors

1. Often lies or makes up stories to get out of trouble
2. Has run away from home overnight or longer
3. Has skipped school
4. Has stolen items, or shoplifted
5. Has been suspended or expelled from school
6. Parents or teachers often complain that he does not listen
7. Rarely finishes work he begins
8. Is easily distracted by noises or people

9. Has difficulty keeping his mind on school work or other areas
10. Impulsive
11. Poor organizer
12. Needs constant supervision at home with chores
13. Needs constant supervision at school
14. Cuts up in class
15. Lacks patience
16. Fidgetiness
17. Disinterest in family or their problems or concerns
18. No attachment to personal belongings or to people
19. Hyperactive
20. Argumentative
21. Has made threats
22. Has been in trouble with the school, police or a juvenile officer
23. Superficial talk
24. Moody pondering about abstract matters
25. Failure to learn from experience
26. Lacks guilt or remorse when such a reaction is appropriate
27. Blames or informs on others to avoid punishment
28. Disobeys the rules at home and school
29. Gets upset and displays his temper if things don't go his way
30. Has little or no regard for the rights of others
31. Shows no respect for authority figures

Early Signs of The Uncaring Child Syndrome

32. Unreliable
33. Oppositional
34. Will insist on doing things his way
35. Sudden mood swings
36. Easily upset
37. Sees life as a bore and rarely admits to having fun
38. Poor judgment
39. Superficial or poor interpersonal relationships
40. Accident prone

In my review of early development patterns of these children, I began to see certain similar patterns that seemed more coincidental. These patterns, due to their subtle and innocuous nature, shall from this point on be referred to as *soft signs*.

When one or more of these soft signs persists for more than a week, we should be alerted to the significance of their meaning. We must first ask: What is happening in our child's life that can account for such a shift in his behavior? Then we can ask: What can we do about it?

Ken

When I first met fourteen-year-old Ken, his parents complained of his lying and stealing, which had gotten him in trouble with the police. Ken's parents were unable to end his antisocial criminal behavior and were considering psychiatric hospitalization.

When Ken was four years old, his parents informed me, he refused to listen to them, needed constant supervision, lacked patience, watched excessive TV, and showed no attachment to his or anyone's personal belongings. Ken had one older brother who his parents said was the opposite, no problem. They began to notice more troublesome behavior when Ken entered the sixth grade. He made failing grades, blamed others to avoid punishment, and lacked guilt whenever confronted for his wrongdoing. The teacher complained he was a "troublemaker" making teaching a chore. He was caught cheating on test, smoking in the boys bathroom and stealing from his classmates. At fourteen, Ken was caught stealing a stereo from a car. It was later learned he had been involved in this activity for almost a year. Suspicion of neighborhood thefts was directed at him.

Initial attempts to gain Ken's cooperation through individual and family therapy failed. Although he was pleasant and cordial, he could not be believed. At no time did he accept the responsibility for his wrongdoings. He blamed his friends for the thefts, indicating he was "only holding the stolen articles for them."

Attempts to change the parent's behavior were met with much frustration. Whenever they made some positive headway, Ken would make them believe he had changed, producing a breakdown in their progress. Finally, they dropped out of therapy and moved him to a private school.

Ken's story is not uncommon. Parents often feel guilty for acting firm. They want the best for their children and fear they will do harm if they are perceived as being unfair and inflexible. They fear their children will leave home, take drugs, and be with "undesirable individuals" Ken's parents expressed these ideas throughout their involvement with me. Ken had always been an "Operator" and able to manipulate his parents. He created the illusion that he needed to be rescued whenever he got in trouble.

Erica

Erica, a twenty-year-old, was brought to me by her parents after she was caught stealing jeans by the store manager. She had been caught several times before. Her parents said she had been a liar since she was nine, was always easily upset, rarely learned from experience, had poor judgment, and was impulsive. When she was six, she was repeatedly caught playing with matches. On many occasions, she lost favorite clothing and put objects in the electric sockets to see the spark. Other soft signs included lacking guilt or remorse when confronted for her wrongdoing, being accident prone, and having little respect for authority figures.

Erica's parents felt that her early behavior was exploratory and were told by her pediatrician, "She will grow out of it. Just continue to provide her with tender, loving care." She did not grow out of her uncaring behavior, she merely grew into adult antisocial criminal behavior.

After determining individual and family therapy were ineffective, special parenting techniques were established. Steps were taken to block Erica's *uncaring behavior*. The parents gave her the choice to abide by the family rules or leave. They had made these threats many times, however, they had not acted on them. Although Erica never changed her behavior, her parent's guilt and anxiety was lessened. Only through a clearer understanding of Erica's early history of *uncaring behavior* and their doing the very best they could for her, were they able to "let go" of their anger and guilt. This process was additionally helped by the parti-cipation in a parent support group.

We've just seen two different outcomes of parental action toward *uncaring* behavior. While Ken's parents chose to allow his behavior to continue by rescuing him and dropping out of therapy, Erica's parents chose to work through the continued difficulties that arose. The point here is that Erica's parents took charge and did not give into their anger and guilt.

We must focus on what can be learned from the experience. If parents are capable of early recognition of soft signs, and develop more effective parenting skills, could there be a more positive outcome? It has been my experience that although *uncaring children* are born with this disorder, the sooner we are able to recognize its existence, the better the chances for recovery. Recovery however, does not mean **cure.** What we can hope to expect from early recognition and identification is extinction of the undesirable behavior associated with the disorder. For example, the child may never truly care about the rights of others, feel the emotional pain of others, experiencing guilt or remorse for his wrongdoings, etc., but the misbehavior associated with these things may possibly be changed or removed. Ken's lying, stealing, and failing grades and Erica's stealing and lying might have been extinguished if their parents had been more skilled in early recognition of soft signs and had adequate skills in parenting the *uncaring child*.

The following is a list of the soft signs for children starting from age two-and-a-half to eighteen years of age.

EARLIEST SOFT SIGNS

Does Not Listen:

I have heard repeatedly from parents who complain that their children, as early as two-years-old, just don't listen to them. They become preoccupied with TV, play, or any number of things. Although frustrated by their children's lack of compliance with rules, parents usually excuse this behavior, attributing it to the age of the child and believe it will improve in good time. The child usually does not return playthings to their proper place, pulls items off store shelves, goes into personal belongings of others, etc.

At age two, Debbie, was often described as a child who "just didn't listen". She seemed to disregard what was expected or what was said. "She has always had a mind of her own and very willful," her mother said. "It just doesn't seem to matter how often or what you say to Debbie, she just won't listen."

Easily Distracted by Noises or People:

This sign has been noted in children as young as two-years-old. These children are easily distracted; and usually have problems with concentration and attention. Although they may be able to concentrate in quiet circumstances, such a child is highly susceptible to interruptions from other stimuli such as nearby movement and "people noises." If the child is trying to read, work a puzzle, or listen to a story being told, any sudden movement nearby or interference rouses a response which he may not be able to control.

Johnny, age three, had great difficulty concentrating. Whenever he was playing, watching TV or being put to bed, he was easily startled by the phone and other noises. His attention would shift to whatever else was going on. His mother said she noticed this behavior before age two in his crib. "When people came into his room," she said, "he would *jump out of his skin* as if he saw a ghost."

Lacks Patience:

Some children become easily frustrated by their lack of "stick-to-it-iveness." They may be playing with a puzzle and are unable to fit the proper pieces together. They quickly abandon their puzzle in favor of another activity. Whenever they face any slight difficulty this pattern appears. However, when a person behaves in this manner repeatedly, it is time to suspect and distrust their motives. We begin to get a picture of how this person deals with conflict, and see the inability to sustain meaningful and healthy human relationships. Few would choose to become a friend to this individual.

Projects Blame:

There are other children who find it difficult to accept responsibility for their actions. When they are confronted by their parents or authority figures, instead of merely accepting the potential consequences, they blame others to "escape" the risk of consequence. In a sense, the child is saying, "I'm not the hostile one, it's them."

Victoria was a child who rarely took the blame for anything. If it wasn't her younger brother's fault, it was her friend's, teacher's, neighbor's, or anyone else who may have been involved. When she was four years old, she blamed her playmate for ruining her dress. In reality, Victoria spilled ink on it. There were innumerable incidents where she blamed others for her own deeds. When confronted, Victoria rarely admitted her blame. Her parents could remember only a few instances of her taking responsibility for her culpability. One example involved accepting the blame for forgetting to inform her father of an important call. Another example involved her forgetting to feed the dog. In these examples, Victoria did admit to forgetting; however, she gave no appearance of genuine concern for the feeling of her dad or the dog.

Disobeys the Rules at Home and School:

In evaluating a child who disobeys the rules, we can categorize his behavior as mild, moderate, or severe. Obviously, the milder the problem, the better the chances for a positive outcome; with more severe the disobedience, more effort is required to discourage its continuance.

Estelle's behavior was marked by leaving the lights on throughout the house, leaving the bathroom dirty, failing to lock the doors, not picking up her room, etc.. Efforts to correct these behaviors were futile. Reminders and sometimes harsh words failed to make things better. By the time she was eleven, Estelle had many expectations of her parents. She, however, did not regard their needs of her as very important. Estelle's behavior was considered to be mild.

Has Little or No Regard for the Rights of Others:

By violating the rights of others, a person proves how little he respects them. Without the capacity of respect, there is little hope of a healthy one-on-one relationship.

At age eight, Michele's continuous "borrowing" of things from her younger sister and mother became a problem. Her lack of concern for their pleas to discontinue this behavior was in vain. There were times where she would use and damage her sister's make-up. Not only would she not tell her about it, she would lie about its use. Many disturbing conflicts arose between the two throughout their relationship at home.

Shows No Respect for Authority Figures:

There is a growing concern in this country for the lack of respect for authority figures, including teachers, politicians, and policeman. A growing number of people are becoming more vocal and physically aggressive towards these figures. Society's moral and ethical standards are being lost. Our children are missing the fundamentals of family and all that it entails.

Dennis, at age seventeen, was taken home by the police. Shortly thereafter, he cursed the policeman for taking the side of his opponent. This type of disrespect for authority figures was first noticed when he was nine years old. He mimicked his teachers and parents. His behavior worsened in high school. Much earlier behavior indicated the presence of *uncaring signs*. At age four, he was demanding, stubborn and had temper outbursts. He displayed little regard for the rights of his playmates and lied.

Difficulty With Play:

During early childhood, each of us develops a need for companionship. A child shows a distinct interest in playmates and chooses them over adults in many situations. These relationships are carried on throughout the normal development of childhood and into adolescence. The soft signs that first appear during early childhood play are in the area of self-play and the sharing of toys. Important themes emerge in the child at these times. Does he display investigative, imitative, and imaginative play? Or is he irritable, crying and demonstrating temper tantrums? Is he interested or disinterested in other children? Is he competitive and well-organized in play while he enjoys peer interaction, or is he not? He may have destructive tendencies with extreme and uncontrollable uncaring behavior, such as lying, stealing, or intentional cruelty to animals.

Crystal, at age four, was already displaying serious signs of problems at play. While playing with her playmates, she grabbed, tossed, and broke the toys. She did not share very well unless she was through playing with each toy. When agitated by her playmates or with her toys, she would pull out the animal's arms, eyes or extremities. Temper outbursts were common.

Marion, at age three-and-a-half, enjoyed playing with her stuffed bear. When playing with other children, she could be seen beating up other children's animals with her bear. She refused to allow anyone else to play with it. She seemed interested in playing with the children, but her rough and disturbing play prevented her attempts. There were times when she seemed gentle and caring and then, without warning, roughshod behavior followed.

Unreliable:

This is a common and perpetual trait in *uncaring children*. They can rarely be counted on for any kind of commitment, and they make excuses for their lack of following through. When confronted for their failure, the *uncaring child* will quickly divert attention from themselves to somewhere else, leaving the confronter dazed, confused, and willing to give them the benefit of the doubt.

Marla, a sixteen-year-old high school student, was rarely counted on by her parents. She once agreed to be home in time to supervise her younger brother. Several hours after the arranged time, Marla came home. Her brother was left unattended. After much confusion and harsh words, Marla blamed her boyfriend and the crowds for coming home late.

Attitude Towards School:

How a child feels about school is important. Often the *uncaring child* has negative feelings toward teachers and the work expected of him. The *uncaring child* will fix blame on anyone and make it seem that they are being picked on unfairly. Ironically, they usually look forward to going to school and socializing with their peers, especially peers of the same type.

Barry always disliked schoolwork. From the time he was six years old, he rarely did homework because he "hated it." His parents said, "He never opens a book to study." Teachers pointed out his tendency to "over-socialize" and his failure to concentrate on studies. Barry's usual complaint was that *his* teachers were "horrible" and the work they gave him was "excessive."

Superficial or Poor Interpersonal Relationships:

In this case, the *uncaring child* is motivated by what he can get. Although for a time he may seem highly charged with caring and concern, he lacks staying power, the will or drive to follow through. He tends to *use* his so-called friends. However, these friends may still consider him to be their best friend. This may be due largely to their own problems with society in general. Problems in this child's relationships will often emerge when the conflicts become too great for him to handle. He often flees from the anxiety, starting a "new life" in a new setting. In doing so, he reenacts the past unhealthy patterns of behavior that got him into the conflict in the first place.

Tatum was eighteen when her world finally fell apart. Her pregnancy and previously strained family relationships made it extremely difficult for her to gain emotional and financial support. Tatum's entire life consisted of lying and manipulation. She never made any attempts to correct damage or emotional pain she inflicted on her loved ones. She avoided resolving any of the conflicts she caused. She showed no remorse or anxiety for her misdeeds nor any concern for those she hurt. She always acted as the victim. Both family and friends were unable to understand her behavior. They spoke of her as "charming, charismatic, yet unreliable, manipulative and sad." Although she seemed to have no trouble making male and female friends, they rarely lasted for more than a few months.

Insists on Doing Things Their Way:

In spite of many attempts to guide and teach your child, they may resist, stubbornly and dogmatically, while insisting they already know how to do or handle something. They tend to show contempt for advice. When they mess up, they make excuses or put the blame elsewhere to cover their failure. This type of behavior is frustrating and maddening, but more significantly, it suggests a child with a narrow and compulsive mind-set and one without the concern for knowledge. They will also accept mediocre performance as a personal standard.

Hal's parents were frustrated by his stubborn personality trait. Regardless of how little he knew, Hal was ready to prove otherwise. Even at age six, his parents recalled his refusal to allow them to help assemble his bike. His stubbornness resulted in some minor damage to the bike. This trait was seen repeatedly when he had difficulty with homework, sports and general activities around the house. Hal would ignore any advice, hints or suggestions. He would do it "his way" in spite of making things more difficult or causing damage.

Sudden Mood Swings:

This behavior is seen in children who are extremely sensitive to both external and internal cues. When they perceive a threat from another person, their moods shift so quickly we usually don't understand the reason for the switch. Sometimes the child appears energetic, self-confident, and cheerful. He makes plans, shows interest in activities, and is warm to people. Then, for no apparent reason, his mood shifts to depression, anger, sulkiness, or discouragement.

Four year old Monica was having fun playing with her doll.

When her playmate moved towards her to play, Monica kicked and expressed rage. A few minutes later, Monica was happy and engaged in play with her playmate.

Sees Life As A Bore and Rarely Admits to Having Fun:

These kids are difficult to please. They appear to be "burnt out" and indifferent to most activities. When they finally appear to be having fun, they don't admit it. They seem to get more satisfaction from acting the poor victim of society rather than deriving pleasure from it.

Sara was taken to Disney World for the day. She pouted and expressed displeasure with the crowds and large lines. While waiting in one line, she complained about wanting to be somewhere else. At the end of the day, and after riding on almost every attraction, she whined and cried that she missed one ride. She would not let up until her parents expressed frustration and anger. By this time, their day was ruined.

Accident Prone:

This is the child who behaves a little more daringly than his peers. He takes unnecessary risks and is the proverbial accident waiting to happen.

Albert was forever hurting himself or breaking something. When he was three, he knocked into lamps and broke dishes. By the time he was twelve, he had broken a finger, a toe, sprained his ankle several times and fallen off his bike on several occasions. His parents were reluctant for him to participate in any activity for fear of his safety.

Risk Taker:

The risk taker is also known as the one who seeks the forbidden, or has a voracious adventurous appetite. He appears unafraid and seeks out what others avoid.

Ivan was the neighborhood dare-devil. He climbed vacant buildings, built underground caves and took risks where others feared to tread. By the time Ivan was eight years old, he had the reputation as "crazy Ivan." He was afraid of nothing.

Has Run Away From Home Overnight or Longer:

Behavior of this sort is more common in the preadolescent and adolescent periods. Continued unresolved problems in the household and at school cause the child to flee rather than to solve the dilemma he has caused. The running away of the Uncaring Child is quite different from that of other children. He is generally without undue anxiety.

After nine-year-old Tommy was grounded for the week, he failed to come home from school. Later that evening, it was learned he had gone to his friend's house to spend the night. Tommy lied to his friend's parents about the alleged abuse he had been receiving from his parents and said he would like to live with them. After investigating the situation, it was discovered that Tommy had also lied about his homework and test scores for the past month. His parents were extremely concerned and engaged a therapist to assist them. They were also considered to be very warm and loving people. Tommy's running away and lying about his parent's alleged abuse was his attempt at making others feel sorry for him. When confronted, he merely put his head down and said, "I don't know why I lied." This was a typical pattern for his unexplained behavior. When at his friend's home, he displayed none of the expected anxiety or fear until his parents came to pick him up. His fear and anxiety however, was due to the confrontation at the moment, not due to the fear of being abused.

Has Skipped School:

Skipping school is common among adolescent *Uncaring Children*. Because they have disconnected themselves from authority figures and their expectations, the consequences of skipping school are usually of minor concern. Depending on their uncaring profile; chameleon, operator, etc. they may be quite clever in their deceptions to skip school or they may show no concern whatsoever for their misdirected behavior.

Throughout the ninth grade, Jordan cut classes and skipped

school entirely. In spite of getting caught on several occasions, his behavior continued. Often he lied about his whereabouts and accused teachers of "having it in for him." He minimized the importance of the classes he cut stating, "I'm getting good grades and felt I could skip class."

Has Stolen Items or Shoplifted:

Unlike the normal child, who may steal or shoplift once, the *Uncaring Child* may derive a sense of pleasure and excitement from the act of stealing. He therefore continues this criminal antisocial behavior without regard for its consequence. He may become preoccupied with the theft. The very thought of the theft is an intense and arousing feeling that he looks to repeat. There seems to be a greater sense of pleasure in performing the act itself than in receiving any profit. These children often come from financially well-off parents. The "chameleon" is one type of the Uncaring Child who can be more easily influenced by his more dominant peer counterparts to steal.

Jill, age seventeen, came from an upper-middle-class family. While in therapy, her preoccupation to steal became quite clear. She stated she got a "high" from the planning to the actual theft. "It was exciting, except getting caught." Throughout her school years, her parents noted, Jill often got involved in behavior initiated by others. On one occasion, Jill and a few of her friends rode their bikes through a shopping mall for a prank. There were many other such episodes instigated by her more dominant playmates.

Has Been Suspended or Expelled From School:

Lack of respect for authority and lack of concern for the consequences for their misbehavior often lead these children to face the possibility of suspension and, on rare occasions, expulsion from school. Through truancy, talking back to teachers, fighting, or generally disrupting their environment, these children more likely to wind up suspended.

By the age of seventeen, Joey had already been suspended six times. Reasons included talking back to teachers, fighting and disruptive behavior in class and on the school grounds. On each occurrence, he blamed the teacher or the students for his actions. He never looked at his own behavior as the possible cause.

Has Made Threats:

Threatening the well-being of others is certainly more serious behavior than skipping school. When behavior reaches this level, it must be stopped. This behavior, besides being a clear and present danger to the safety and well-being of others, could also be harmful to the child itself.

At age fourteen, Pam was suspended for fighting in school. When she got home, she told her mother she was going to kill the other girl for getting her into trouble. On two other occasions, Pam made threats towards others who had "offended" her. Although the rage eventually diminished, Pam was unwilling and unable to appreciate her role in making problems worse.

Has Been In Trouble with The School, Police, or a Juvenile Officer:

This type of behavior is exhibited through not doing homework, disrespect, fighting, talking back, stealing, drug and alcohol use, making threats, etc. A persistent and blatant pattern of Uncaring behaviors is usually associated with the act. If a child winds up with a juvenile authority for example, you can be fairly certain that a patter of Uncaring behaviors existed prior to his current dilemma. Additionally, this type of child is almost always in conflict with his parents.

Mason was stopped by the police for speeding. He became unruly and rude to the police officer when questioned about his expired drivers license. As a result of his behavior, he was taken to the police station. It was learned he had three additional speeding and four moving violations in the past year-and-a-half. His parents indicated his use of foul language, disrespect and problems at school.

Superficial Talk:

This is a way of avoiding basic issues. Instead of discussing important concerns, the child may spend a great deal of time talking about topics of the day, his friends, or past experiences. There is little significance in what he is saying, and he may go on talking about anything that has little bearing on the problems at hand.

Since the age of eight, Jane seemed to talk around issues. She could never be pinned down to the topic at hand. For example, when she failed to clean her room, she stated she would "get to it," and then discussed her broken stereo, friend's new dog or other unrelated thoughts. Her parents remarked how difficult and frustrating it was to deal with any single issue. When it came to discussing her progress in school, her talk was focused on her improved performance since the last report card. Then she talked about her "bad" teachers, rotten school, clothing, vacations, etc.

Expecting Others to Indulge Him:

Some children put little of themselves into relationships. They are takers, not givers. They expect parents to provide them with the latest fad clothing, give them undue spending money, and constantly offer them special presents. When they are asked to help out with chores or the like, they act indignant or "just to busy."

Winnie was a child who expected her parents to provide her with the latest clothes and spending money. When she was sixteen, she expected a new car and money to buy insurance. During her lifetime, there was rarely a time when her parents could count on her for anything. She could be found sitting on the couch, watching TV, going to the refrigerator, leaving the house when the family was working on chores or other projects. She was considered lazy by all.

Dismisses Usual Recognition of Good Deeds:

Although these children are given recognition for good deeds and treated with special rewards, they have a need to demonstrate their misery by avoiding the feelings of success. This is largely due to poor self-esteem and an intolerable sense of failure. When they do accept recognition for their good deeds, they quickly seize the opportunity to gain a manipulative foothold.

When Bobbie's parents told her how wonderfully she did on her test score, she asked for fifteen dollars and permission to borrow their car. Her parents felt that whenever they praised her, she would take that opportunity to get something in return from them. "She never just said thanks." She rarely looked pleased at the praise and responded by pouting or with anger. It was their feeling Bobbie didn't want to be expected to complete anything - so her response was usually contrary.

Manipulative:

Attempts to influence by deception and to put something over on the other person are a source of satisfaction for this *uncaring child* when he is successful. When he is not, he may display contempt or make other demands until he *is* successful. He feels that he deserves what he is attempting to gain and experiences no guilt for his actions. Because he feels deprived and victimized, he is able to rationalize his manipulative activity as being appropriate.

Joshua became angry and gloomy when his father denied him the use of the car. Continuing his efforts to make his father feel guilty, Joshua told his therapist that he was almost always successful in "turning" his parents around. Although his parents felt they were being "used," they continued to give into his "needs." They rationalized that, "Josh wasn't much different than most other sixteen year old boys. After all, he wasn't doing drugs."

Knack for Forgetfulness:

When a parent asks her child, "Why haven't you done your homework?" or "Why haven't you taken out the trash?" he replies, "I forgot." This is probably the most common complaint I hear from parents when they describe areas of frustration with their children. We begin to wonder if their is an epidemic of cognitive hearing deficits going around the country.

Denise agreed to take the trash out on Tuesday and Friday evening. Unless her parents reminded her, she failed to perform this task half of the time. Her usual response was "I forgot."

Poor School Grades:

One of the most useful soft signs, especially for preadolescents and adolescents, that can serve as a red flag of concern is declining school grades. This is measurable behavior that cannot be disputed. Many times, however, the child will insist his poor grades are a teacher error or the result of a child/teacher conflict. Or, he promises to "do better." This is where parents should take special notice. Poor grades should serve as a reference point that may indicate the need to look more deeply into their child's world.

Melinda's first problem with school grades was in the fourth grade. When she reached middle school, she was getting C's and D's. Whenever her parents approached her regarding her progress, she replied, "I'm doing better this semester," or "my teacher made a mistake." There was rarely a time when Melinda accepted the responsibility for her sub-average grades.

For the purpose of early prevention and treatment of children who may be exhibiting the *Uncaring Child Syndrome*, the early warning signs (soft signs) are offered for consideration. There are many varieties of and similarities among the maladaptive behavioral patterns of *Uncaring Children*. If we are better warned, we are better prepared to deal more effectively. Until now, *Uncaring Children* have had the upper hand. They have been in control, and played havoc with the family structure. Parents have lost power and their ability to parent. Without a complete understanding of the *Uncaring Child Syndrome*, most parents remain defenseless and ill-equipped to neutralize their child's destructive nature. The recognition of early warning signs adds to parents' weaponry. Fortification of the family's position is, at last, made possible through this knowledge. Parents can clearly identify misbehavior through early recognition of soft signs. When they are properly identified, early intervention can be effected. Through early intervention, there is a greater opportunity for changing unhealthy patterns of behavior the better the outcome. The longer the misbehavior is present, the more difficult it is to change.

5

Follow The Leader

"There are times when parenthood seems like nothing but feeding the mouth that bites you."

Peter De Oris

    Peer pressure, TV, folk and rock stars, religious and political leaders are all credited as major influences in swaying public opinion. Although we recognize our ability to sort out information and make informed choices, it's impressive how certain people have the ability to influence others. Children follow the misguided suggestions of particular playmates who lead them into trouble. In spite of otherwise good judgment they mindlessly follow a strong lead. When *uncaring children* follow the lead of *uncaring children*, we have a combination of dangerous elements that can lead to tragic *consequences.*

    Have you ever noticed how some people seem to have unusual ability to gain attention and influence others? They have that certain unexplained quality called charisma, charm or power. Other people seem to follow their lead as if they were hypnotized.

Power or dominance is the focus of this chapter because it may hold the key that unlocks the mysteries of unexplained behaviors, especially those behaviors that seem unmotivated, without direction, or even dangerous.

Many scientific studies[24] compare human and animal behavior. Unfortunately, the observations and conclusions from these studies have yet to be put in full use. When we observe the behavior of chickens, we note the presence of the "pecking order." A hierarchy of dominance/power is obvious in the group. The chickens with the most power are allowed to peck the ones with the least power. We see the same phenomenon in almost all the animal species.

Maslow[25] examined relationships among monkeys. He saw that the monkeys were preoccupied with sex and that they did not discriminate between the sexes. Male monkeys mounted other males, and females mounted other females. Of course, both sexes also mounted the opposite sex. Maslow concluded that the highly dominant apes mounted the less dominant ones, regardless of sex.

Dominant and subdominant behavior in the animal kingdom has also been documented in the work of Diane Fossey[26] who fought to save the African mountain gorilla from extinction and Jane Goodall[27] the naturalist, who demonstrated this dominance in her observations of the apes of Africa.

With regard to humans, the Korean War produced an amazing, yet similar discovery. During the war, not one American ever escaped his Korean captors. The Koreans were able to pick out those prisoners they felt were dominant and place them in quarters separate from their subdominant peers. Once the subdominant prisoners were not under the influence of the dominant ones, they remained easy to control.[28] How did this happen?

From extensive psychiatric examinations, it was determined that the prisoners fell into six categories.[29] Three categories accounted for "outright collaborator" behavior (13%).[30]

A fourth category, the largest "was made up of men who chose what seemed to them to be the path of least resistance" (75%).[31] They complied on the surface, but were able to protect themselves from becoming involved in more serious collaborations. They were known to prisoners for "playing it cool."[32]

The last two groups fell into two categories of reactionaries

(13%), equivalent to the number of direct collaborators. The study divided the reactionaries into two groups. The first group included those with long histories of previous authority conflicts. These people were people who had life long problems accepting authority. Their army records underscored this fact. They were not seen as leaders of men nor were they respected for their behavior. With regard to the other reactionaries Kinkead stated,

> The other group of reactionaries were those who were respected and well integrated individuals who know how to use their intelligence constructively; how to work with all sorts of men, and how to influence them to gain a goal of importance to them all, how to use the respect they had earned from their prisoners to quietly sabotage the indoctrination program. These men were true heroes of the prison camps.

The Korean captors were able to understand their influence on the prisoners. When the indoctrination program began, these men were isolated, sent to their camps and given hard labor details.

Another account, the Wang Report[33] was a document describing basic Communist techniques used in China and then again in Korea on our GIs. Of significant importance in this report was the ability of the captors to identify the least resistive candidates for indoctrination. They found that the most cooperative were the young enlisted men of higher socioeconomic status.

The significance of this finding is in the idea of influencing the young. This example of Korean indoctrination may help us understand more clearly the suscep-tibility of our youth to follow the destructive antisocial signals of their peers and society.

Why is this dominant theory so vitally important in the field of human development, especially when dealing with children's behavior? How can we best use this information when faced with our children's disruptive behavior at home or at school?

The answers are as fascinating as the questions. First, let us return to the earlier comparison of humans to other forms in the animal kingdom. When we are forced to live in confined quarters, such as in jails, ghettos, etc., we behave much like the Maslow's monkeys in the Bronx Zoo. There is an increase in domestic violence, sexual acting out, frustration, and gang participation. The child, like the monkey, fits somewhere on the domestic scale; his peers force him to remain there. Like an actor in a Shakespearean play, he remains true to his role. This role becomes his badge in his surroundings. He takes on the characteristics and mannerisms that are dictated by the more dominant personalities in his social group. His role becomes strengthened and reinforced by the positive acknowledgments of his group. Without realizing it, he becomes a mindless, brainwashed member of a common group process.

Jim Jones

If we need to be reminded of this phenomenon, we only have to look at Jim Jones, the preacher who led hundreds of followers to commit mass suicide, in Guyana; or Charles Manson, the brutal murderer and leader of a cult in southern California. In each case, a clearly defined dominant leader dominated the less dominant followers.

On November 18, 1978, we were informed of the hideous tragedy in Guyana. The mass murder-suicide at Jonestown and the name of Jim Jones and the People's Temple will never fade from most of our memories. An incident of frightful and catastrophic proportion took place.[34]

When I first heard of the Guyana tragedy, I wondered how many people could be so easily influenced by one person. It was difficult to comprehend how individuals from many diverse walks of life could surrender themselves to the yearnings of Jim Jones. My first reaction to the slaughter was that these individuals had little will of their own and were rejects of society. I was informed, however, that this was indeed not the case. There was a diversity of class, intellect, skills and wealth within the membership of the cult. Questions continued to plague me regarding the submission of so many people to one leader, one voice, one command. What could possibly make individuals obey such destructive demands in such a mindless and dangerous fashion? What were the forces at play that could explain this phenomenon?

We were forced to acknowledge the fact that people from all

walks of life can be brainwashed and dominated to perform the most horrifying and repulsive acts of violence on others and to themselves. Here we had a religious leader, whose previous behavior had demonstrated a love for humanity and love for humankind, that turned his humility and love to antisocial criminal brutality.

Charles Manson

Having studiously followed the Manson saga, I was amazed by the dominance and control he held over his followers. I first heard about the Manson murders in 1970, but it wasn't until 1974, when *Helter Skelter*[35] was first published, that I became interested in the issues related to domination. This book explored, in depth, a person who had the power to and direct his evil thoughts at those under his influence. His followers would, mindlessly and without hesitation, commit some of the most ruthless criminal acts known to American history.

In *Helter Skelter* the author, Bugliosi, offers us an unusual glance into the dark mind of Charles Manson.

Manson believed:

> Fear is beneficial . . . Fear is the catalyst of action. It is the energizer, the weapon built into the game in the beginning, enabling a being to create an effect upon himself, to spur himself on to new heights and to brush aside the bitterness of failure.[36]

Manson needed to be around weak people he could use. He would repeat phrases to program them while instilling fear, making them believe the Manson family was the only one left to care. He was said to have charisma and an incredibly persuasive power. He had strong beliefs which followed Nietzche's philosophy which says: "Women are inferior to men; the white race is superior to all the other races; it is not wrong to kill if the end is right" [37]

Manson was a person who also knew how to convince his followers that he had magical powers. His con man techniques were effective in supplying them with what they needed. Drugs were used as an effective agent to make his followers more compliant and follow his commands.

Manson once said:

> You can convince anybody of anything if you just push it at them all of the time. They may not believe it 100 percent, but they will still draw opinions from it, especially if they have no other information to draw their opinions from.[38]

Manson became the only source of information to his followers. He managed to create an environment that totally conformed to his reality. He created a family that loved and cared and killed.

> the group obeys certain natural tendencies; however, these tendencies were not toward spontaneous creation, but toward mindless repetition.[39]

The relationship between Manson and his followers as well as Jim Jones and his followers is the strangest and most important aspect of the dominant versus subdominant theme. It is this relationship, this merger of two different forces, that can generate the spark that creates either pointless brutality or beneficial and constructive deeds. Both Jones and Manson represent only the negative forces of destruction; but positive, constructive relationships do exist to produce healthy outcomes. Our children, for instance, are led by teachers, church leaders, parents, therapists, politicians, and the like, who help them. It is difficult indeed for any of us to sort out and determine what is good or bad advice. How are we to know what leaders, religious or otherwise, are good or bad, or will turn bad if given to much power? And what is to much power? The peculiar relationship between a highly dominant person and his subordinates can produce various concerns. What are the factors that enable one person to have power over another? How do these individuals meet? What are the conditions that cause a person to act out his aggressive and destructive tendencies? I raise these questions, and others, in order to look more closely at the workings of the dominant and subdominant mind.

Robert Ardrey, the American author of *African Genesis*, stated,[40] "In any group of eight or ten, random chance would dictate that one at least had superior capacities" He went on to say: "So it may be that what seems insanely small group of a dozen or twenty or a hundred individuals may with the desperate dedication seek to force an all human populations acceptance of the group's illusion." [41]

Maslow's Dominance Study

Abraham Maslow,[42] the scientist who determined that the women he studied could be categorized into three groups. The first group was labeled *highly dominant*. These women were in great need of sexual excitement and involvement in highly sexual activities. They experimented freely with sexual partners, including other women. These highly dominant women would often choose highly dominant males in order to fulfill their sexual needs. They had no need for close, intimate relationships.

Medium dominant women tended to be more gentle. They were more traditional, caring women who were looking for the more gentle and sensitive male to a highly dominant one. Although they enjoyed sex, they were much less experimental than the *highly dominant* females.

Maslow discovered that the *low dominant* females disliked sex and thought of it as dirty. The only reason they chose to have sex was for having children.

Although this study is far from complete in its attempt to clarify the dominant and lessor dominant personality, it does raise questions about the power related to dominance and its influence.

What this study also suggests is that individuals have their own personal dominant-subdominant blueprint. With careful observations, we might be able to understand why and how people relate with each other as they do. This is especially important in the relationships between the *high dominant* (master) and the *low dominant* (slave) personality. The master/slave relationship is one of the most fascinating. It is this relationship that breeds the potential for Uncaring and antisocial criminal behavior. The *lower dominant* partner is easily manipulated because of his need for approval and fear of losing his more *highly dominant* mate.

Characteristics of High Dominance

Sean had many characteristics of the highly dominant individual. They are as follows:

1. little regard for what people thought of him
2. temper outbursts
3. aggressive
4. stubborn
5. highly motivated to achieve his personal goals
6. no respect for others
7. honesty is thought of as a lessor value
8. many friends but easily disliked
9. has charm and charisma to attract others to follow him
10. lacks sensitivity and regard for the rights or feelings of others
11. has firm and unbending beliefs
12. a skillful manipulator
13. lacks guilt or remorse
14. arrogant
15. highly persuasive
16. thrill seeker
17. extremely sensitive in intuitive in knowing what people want

Lindholm[43] discusses the presence of a "central and inspiring figure to rouse them (the dominated) to action; a stone needs to be thrown, the organizing gesture made." Tarde[44] wrote, "Human beings are portrayed as unconscious puppets who mechanically imitate whatever arouses them from their torpor (stupor)." Freud feared the charismatic leader and the power he could wield over the populous.[45]

What we have learned thus far is two-fold; first, there are those who have special, inborn abilities to control others, and second, there are those who can be controlled. What will be the most useful for parents to take from this chapter is information that will clearly identify the characteristics and personality traits of the *highly dominant* versus the *lower dominant* types. Although I don't believe having special knowledge of these traits can have much bearing on changing them, it might help prevent problems from occurring.

For example, your eight-year-old boy is playing with several youths in the neighborhood. Spotting the *highly dominant* traits of one of his playmates, you become more alert and cautious in allowing your son to continue in this relationship. This would be especially true if your son has a *low dominant* personality. The obvious potential for the master/slave relationship is present. The comparison of high dominant to low dominant characteristics presented later in this chapter will help you spot and identify your childrens' dominant and submissive traits and can be beneficial in preventing possible harm. Like the asthmatic or hearing impaired child, the *low dominant* person is like the prey of the lion. He is, and may always be, at risk.

Paul

Paul was seventeen when first brought to my attention. His parents told me that he was a dutiful young boy throughout his childhood. He was especially close to his mother, spending a great deal of time with her when his father was at work. His parents said, "Paul was a good boy, sensitive and sweet."

When he was sixteen, he met Trish, a girl three years his senior. He fell deeply and madly in love. At first his parents offered no resistance to his first love; however, they began to sense their son's personality change. He became argumentative, demanding, and hostile. As the relationship intensified, Paul leveled attacks on his mother who was "phony and stupid."

After meeting this family in therapy, I was convinced that Paul's complaints were unfounded. When asked about his accusations about his mother, he would repeat the same phrase, "She's a fake and a phony." Or he would say, "She's sick," or "She's stupid." When I pressed him to expand on his statements, he brought up vague references to his early childhood, when he was about three years old and his mother was touching his penis. He also recalled how his mother embarrassed him by kissing him in front of his friends when he was fifteen years of age. Other than these complaints, Paul was unable to elaborate on any reasons why he was so greatly disturbed at this time in his life. His only wish was to leave his parents' home, live with his girlfriend, yet continue to be supported by his parents until he was fully independent.

When I met Paul's girlfriend Trish, I was impressed by the energy she radiated while attempting to convince me of Paul's need to leave his parents. She described the problems that Paul was having with his parents and his need to "break away from their grasp." She indicated that they were "overbearing" and "used him." She emphasized that they had rarely paid any attention to him while he was growing up, spending all of their time either with their business or traveling. She described Paul as coming from deviant parents who "never" loved him. She further stated his mother was "sick," because "she smothered him, keeping him from growing up."

Because of the complexity of this rapidly disintegrating situation, I called for a family meeting. As I spoke with Paul's twenty-year-old brother and fourteen-year-old sister, I was impressed by their concern for Paul and their warmth for their parents. They were articulate and gave me the impression that Paul, although a sensitive and caring boy, spent a great deal of time alone in his room and didn't have many friends. As a child with his friends, he would give them his toys, money, or any other personal belongings to keep their friendship. His siblings also indicated that Paul "worshiped" his mother, that until he fell in love with Trish, they were inseparable. He was very dependent on her for making appointments, schedules, homework, etc.. He also needed much reassurance and praise. He was always concerned how people thought of him, fearing he was disliked and that he would never have friends.

What is most beneficial about reading Paul's story is the understanding it brings regarding *lower dominant* personality characteristics. Paul never seemed to have an identity of his own. His personality appeared to be part of another person's personality, much like the "chameleon" in Chapter 2. In other words, Paul needed others in order to feel whole. During his early life, he shared his personality with his mother. His over-dependence on her, his need of approval, and her unintentional feeding into it did little to develop in him a healthier means of relating.

He was clearly a *lower dominant* young man who was later lured by a woman's highly dominant influence. Trish was able to convince Paul that his parents were "bad" and she was "good." Paul was "madly" in love and lust with her, so he was very much afraid of losing her if he did not leave his parents. She presented herself as the only one who truly understood and loved him and could help free him of his "bad" parents. Paul seemed helplessly and hopelessly dominated but felt a great deal of power, as long as he did his girlfriend's bidding. Extremely important during the initial phase of Paul's relationship with Trish was his attempt to commit suicide when she threatened to leave him. Paul told me that she was leaving because of an argument they had about her considering going back to her previous boyfriend. She was also angry about his continuing to live with his parents.

Shortly after Paul moved in with Trish, he dropped out of therapy. Paul's parents were left with a feeling of guilt and sorrow. Although they were able to reestablish a relationship with him, he would never visit them without Trish being present. And, when there was contact, it was brief. Paul continued to accept financial support for car payments, insurance and other living expenses. The parents stated they felt if they discontinued their support, they would lose him altogether.

Linda

Linda was eight years old when she began to demonstrate serious problems at school. Her teachers told her parents she was "bossy, stubborn, aggressive, and creating disturbances in the classroom." One teacher told them of an incident where Linda persuaded two of her classmates to play a trick on another girl. This prank resulted in the victim having her birthday watch broken. The teacher indicated this was not the first such incident Linda had orchestrated.

Linda's parents said she was a strong willed young girl who had been difficult to raise. She was "always" arguing with her siblings. They said she "has" to be right. In spite of her aggressiveness with her peers, she seemed to have friends at her door.

What was being disclosed was the profile of a highly dominant and possibly *Uncaring* female. She was relatively indifferent to what people said or felt about her behavior. She showed little regard for the rights of others. She had highly adapted manipulative skills; and, she had a certain charismatic charm with her peers. In all reports from those in contact with her, "Linda had to be the boss."

Apparently, when *higher dominant* and *lower dominant* people get together, there is always the possibility of lethal interaction. The *higher dominant* is the master and the *lower dominant* is the slave. If the higher dominant happens to be an *Uncaring* individual, it is easy to imagine the potential for disaster. Combining the *Uncaring* dominant and the lower dominant can produce great harm.

On the following page, you will find features that may be helpful in detecting the differences between higher dominant (master) and lower dominant (slave) characteristics. This comparative material is taken from my thirty-four years of clinical experience, data collection, case material, reading, clinical profiles and personal investigation.

Comparisons of the Higher/Lower Dominant Child

HIGHER DOMINANT UNCARING CHILD	LOWER DOMINANT UNCARING CHILD
Usually takes the responsibility to make the decisions	Rarely assumes the responsibility to make the decisions
Has little regard for what people thinks of him/her	Is very much concerned about what others feel

Temper outbursts can be expected when he/she doesn't get their way	Will usually yield to the more highly dominant when there is a question
Is likely to be more aggressive	Is likely to be less aggressive
Stubborn	Much less stubborn
Highly motivated to achieve his personal goals	Poorly motivated towards goal achievement
Rarely shows anxiety	Shows anxiety more often
Is very selective in giving others respect	Is very envious and often gives respect to others
Highly sexual and feels free to experiment sexually	Feels sex is filthy unless it is for the bearing of
Honesty is a lessor value	Honesty is more important, but when under control of a highly dominant person, the person is easily manipulated to be dishonest

May have many friends but is easily disliked	Has few friends and is not often liked
Usually prefers to be alone but will choose to be with others as long as they follow his lead	Usually prefers to be with others
Lacks sensitivity and regard for the feelings of others	Is very sensitive to how others may feel
Has firm and unbending beliefs	Has loose and bending beliefs
Very demanding	Not very demanding
A skillful manipulator	Easily manipulated
Lacks the usual guilt and remorse	Experiences undue guilt and remorse
Has the charm and charisma to attract others	Lacks the ability to attract others
Tends to be arrogant	Tends to be humble

Is very sensitive and intutive in knowing what people want	Is very sensitive to giving what the other person wants and needs
Highly persuasive	Easily persuaded
Thrill Seeker	Avoids thrill seeking unless in the control of a more highly dominant person
Is very sensitive and intutive in knowing what people want	Is very sensitive to giving what the other person wants and needs

6

Alcohol, Drugs and Crime

*"Habitual intoxication is the epitome
of every crime."*

Jerrold (1803-57)

    The purpose of this chapter is to distinguish drug and alcohol behavior from the behavior of the *Uncaring Child*. Is the adolescent's abuse of drugs or alcohol an early warning sign of uncaring and/or antisocial criminal behavior, or merely an illness associated with the substance abuse? This chapter explores the immense drug and alcohol abuse problem as well as the moral and social problems resulting from our children's indulgence and abuse.
    First, let us look at the effects drug and alcohol abuse has on the child and society. The typical user/abuser uses the drugs to get high - to feel good. As drugs are everywhere, the child has no difficulty obtaining them. Alcohol, marijuana, cocaine and crack are the most popular and the easiest drugs to acquire.[46] Many of the children

answer yes to the question, "Do you know of anyone in your school or neighborhood that has or is using or selling drugs?"

The general consensus today is that anyone can be addicted.[47] There is no personality type for the alcoholic or drug abuser. There is evidence however, that a person has a greater chance of becoming addicted to alcohol and drugs if one or both parents are an alcoholic.

The most widely abused drug today is alcohol. That is probably due to its legality. Many of the kids that abuse alcohol are also using other chemicals. These at-risk children show signs of emotional problems, i.e., anxiety, anger, rage, depression and psychosis. I have often heard from teenagers that they believe marijuana is harmless. They insist there is no conclusive evidence to prove it is dangerous. In fact, they believe it is much less dangerous than alcohol. My observations, however, paint a different picture. The children I see who are using marijuana usually fit into the category of those who have lost interest and motivation in their school work and relationships with their parents. One of my sixteen year old patients, a marijuana user, said to me, "If you think me or my friends are going to contribute to anything positive to this world, then think again." Prior to his drug use, his parents told me that he was a good boy who was very affectionate. Unfortunately, due to his continual use of drugs, it was impossible to reach any of his positive traits. The drugs had taken over his thinking and attitude. Of course there is the inherent danger of driving while drinking or drugging. The danger to oneself and others goes without saying. Sadly, the abuser's judgment and insight into the potential danger is grossly impaired. And of course, it is illegal to use these drugs. The resultant cost to personal property and life is enormous.

The effect that intoxication has on the *uncaring* individual is the lowering of their resistance to criminal impulses. While intoxicated, they are less likely to care about the rights of others or the dangerous outcome of their behavior. Even in everyday, "normal" conflicts, the *uncaring* type personality can be lethal. This *uncaring*, unloving person who lacks good judgment and guilt can become harmful and dangerous with the addition of alcohol or drugs. Let us suppose an *uncaring* individual's girl friend left him. His anger and rage becomes intensified with the use of intoxicants. The drugs or alcohol reduce his ability to control his impulses to do harm. With an already impaired ability to have good judgment, he acts out his impulse to do harm without any consideration of the consequences. This lethal combination of intoxicants and *uncaring* traits give rise to his criminal attitude and behavior.

How does the *uncaring* and drinking/drugging combination differ from that of a caring child who drinks or drugs? Although many criminal types use intoxicants, many drinkers/druggers are not criminals, and not all of the crimes associated with alcohol are committed by antisocial criminals. In the following example we see how Mitchell goes from *uncaring* to antisocial behavior. This is the kind of movement we want to avoid.

Mitchell

Because alcohol addiction creates a powerful hold on the abuser, this hold must be broken prior to any attempt to remediate *uncaring* behavior.

Mitchell was eighteen years old when he was arrested for the fifth time, for burglary and grand theft. When he was arrested he was intoxicated on alcohol and other chemicals. Although the intoxicants could be blamed for reducing his control to commit the crimes, they could not be the cause of his repeated criminal activity. His drinking/drugging behavior was an extension of his criminal pursuits. Like most individuals who use and abuse substances, Mitchell used alcohol and drugs for the purpose of pleasure seeking, relieving tension and stress, cheering bad moods and helping with sleep. He felt more sociable, sexual and outgoing when under the influence. Sadly, due to his criminal antisocial personality, Mitchell's involvement in drug and alcohol abuse only contributed to increasing his criminal impulses. His continued use of these substances helped maintain and even increased his antisocial criminal activities.

Lawrence

Lawrence's story is a good illustration of the difference between the *uncaring* individual and the alcoholic. Lawrence was eighteen years old when he was arrested for drunk driving. He had no other criminal record. His drinking problem began when he was thirteen years old. It caused many hardships with his family and friends. Yet during the entire course of his problem with alcohol, he was never involved in any illegal behavior. In fact, his guilt and remorse was quite apparent after every drinking episode. Everyone who knew Lawrence spoke of him in glowing, but sad, terms. They said when he abstained from alcohol he was caring, sensitive and loving. The picture of the alcoholic is sometimes confusing. His anger, lies, unreliability, personality and mood swings are not much different than that of the *uncaring child*. *The major difference is in his capacity for guilt and remorse when he has fallen off the wagon. The "uncaring" person often shows no concern for the serious harm he has caused himself or others.* Also, the alcoholic, like Lawrence, does not have a history of *uncaring* behavior, (skipping school, rebelling against authority, running away), prior to his alcohol abuse.

The chance of the basic alcoholic eventually responding to treatment is usually much better than that of the alcoholic *uncaring* individual. It should be made clear, however, that the alcoholic can cause the same amount of devastation to his family, friends, relatives and society as does the *uncaring* individual or antisocial criminal. This is largely due to the extent of the crime committed by either one. It is certainly fair to say, the basic alcoholic, under the influence of intoxicants, can rob, steal and even kill. Although alcohol or drug abuse does not make a person an antisocial criminal, it is quite possible for the person under the influence, to commit an antisocial criminal act.

It is difficult enough to attempt to deal with *uncaring children* without the influence of intoxicants; but, with the added problem of use/abuse, the treatment of the *uncaring child* becomes a nightmare. It would be foolish to think of dealing with *uncaring* behavior before extinguishing the drinking/drugging behavior.

I recall a single parent and his girlfriend coming to me for advice for his nineteen year old boy. The young man had a history of lying, stealing, disrespect for authority, lacking motivation, truancy and failing grades. During the two years prior to our association he become addicted to alcohol and marijuana. The father wanted me to help stop his son's misbehavior and marijuana use. He felt it would be alright, however, for his son to continue drinking as drinking is socially acceptable.

In treating this condition, it is essential that you deal with the addictive areas first. Addiction to alcohol and drugs must be eliminated in order for the *uncaring behaviors* to be addressed. It would be like treating a suicidal spouse for his/her marital problem before first securing the person's safety. Likewise, working on marital issues would be useless if the person committed suicide. Working on *uncaring behavior* would equally be useless if the person continued his drinking/drugging.

Crack, probably the most addictive drug today, is wrecking havoc on our kids throughout the United States. Crack is a purified and an extremely addictive form of cocaine. Its low price, wide-spread availability and immediate, intense gratification makes it the most desirable drug in the marketplace. All of the drug abuse specialists agree, once you use it, it uses you.[48]

Mark

Mark had the world at his fingertips. He came from a hard working middle class family. Other than exhibiting moderate hyperactivity and a reading problem, Mark and his family got through his early years and schooling without a great deal of difficulty. Mark was very mechanical and bright. He followed in his father's footsteps heading toward a career in the plumbing field. He had been working along side his father for almost a year when he explored crack for the first time. Within a few days, Mark was lying, argumentative and highly anxious. After a month, he began to steal from his parents and pawn their personal belongings. His personality began to change rapidly. He made excuses for not going to work. His hostility turned into rage. It wasn't until Mark came home bloodstained early one morning that his parents knew he was in serious trouble. Mark said he was in a car accident after leaving his girlfriends house. They later discovered that was a lie. They began to find drug paraphernalia, i.e., pipes, baggies, rolling paper and seeds. A medical examination revealed high blood pressure, rapid pulse rate and dehydration. A blood test for drug screening was performed with positive results. He admitted to using marijuana, alcohol and crack; he agreed to go to counseling.

Alcohol, Drugs and Crime

The counseling efforts that followed were extremely painful and almost tragic. Mark had six backslides during the first six months of treatment. For the first month, I saw him twice a week. After several relapses, he agreed to enter a drug rehabilitation program for one month. During that period, and the months that followed, Mark continued to have short episodes when he used coke and crack. Finally, after his parents reported him missing for three days, he was found severely beaten. When he was admitted to the hospital emergency room, his physical condition was so deteriorated, they barely kept him alive. During the months that followed, Mark and his parents endured a great deal of worry, frustration, financial decay and anger. Fortunately, the outcome was positive with Mark going back to school and eventually getting his contractor's license. Mark's abuse of crack and cocaine continues to haunt him today. He still has a desire to use crack. He fights the powerful effects of the drug's addictive qualities every day. He indicates he can smell and taste crack in spite of not using it for over a year. This smell and taste phenomenon has been reported to me on several occasions from those who have been addicted to crack.

Although Mark could not be classified an *uncaring child*, his drug related behavior was much the same. He lied, stole and had little regard for the rights and feelings of others. One thing was different, however; he experienced and expressed an enormous amount of guilt and shame. Unfortunately, when the need arose, he sought out the source of the drug without regard for those he loved most and those who most loved him. He would lie, steal, borrow, beg and humiliate himself for it. He had stolen the jewelry his mother was given by her mother in Russia. Although he was aware of the tremendous sentimental value it held for her, he took it anyway. Mark indicated he had no control over his addiction or what he might do to get the drug.

Let us now attempt to clarify the differences between the *uncaring drinker/drugger* from that of the *non-uncaring drinker/drugger*. First, there does not appear to be any typical alcoholic or drug abuser profile. However, there are significant differences between the *uncaring drinking/drugging* profile and the *non-uncaring drinking/ drugging* profile. These differences are as follows:

Drinking/Drugging Profile

Uncaring Drinker/Drugger	**Non-Uncaring Drinker/Drugger**
History of misbehavior usually prior to the alcohol/drug abuse, i.e., lying, stealing, may truancy, conflicts with authority, running away from home, conflict with police.	Uncaring behavior follows drug and alcohol use. Criminal actions occur under the influence of drugs or alcohol.
Lack of guilt, remorse or shame for their uncaring acts.	Shows guilt, remorse or shame for his uncaring actions.
The use of drugs and alcohol did not cause his uncaring misbehavior.	Drug and alcohol abuse may cause his uncaring acts.
Difficulty establishing a career.	Establishing a career is more predictable.
Early onset of drug and alcohol use/abuse.	Early or later onset of drug/alcohol use/abuse.
Drug and alcohol intake is is more likely associated with associated criminal behavior.	Drug and alcohol intake less likely to be with criminal behavior.
Impulsiveness.	Impulsiveness.
Lack of good judgment and insight.	Lack of good judgment and insight.
Problems with work and personal life.	Problems with work and personal life.

Likely to abuse spouse and family with or without the intake of drugs or alcohol.	Likely to abuse spouse and family with or without the intake of drugs or alcohol.

The effects of drug and alcohol abuse do not only reach those who have the choice to explore their evil offering. There are those that are born into its ever reaching grip. Everyday infants are born with either an addiction or with a propensity toward behavior that makes normal child development difficult.

Mary Ann

Mary Ann was a hyperactive, stubborn, demanding and ill-tempered six-year-old. During the first year of life, she refused to be held, cuddled or loved. She cried at her mother's attempts to breast feed her. She was equally impossible to bottle feed, spitting out almost all of her formula.

Mary Ann's mother was an intravenous drug user and addicted to alcohol before, during and after the pregnancy. Mary Ann was born prematurely due to her mother's bleeding during pregnancy. She was also a fussy baby, screaming most of the time.

Mary Ann's mother lost custody after the first year when her grandparents took over custody. During the following years, she became increasingly more stubborn, demanding and mischievous. She would not listen to her grandparents and made their life miserable.

When I first say Mary Ann, I found her to be quite exasperating. She got into everything in my office without any regard for their value or harm to her. She would explore electric chords and sockets and jump on the furniture. Any attempts to caution or stop her resulted in further exploration, contempt or both. Her grandparents informed me of her demand to sleep in their room rather than her own. She refused to go to bed at the usual time. Moreover, she would not eat most of the food they prepared or share any of her playthings with her peers. Their attempts to control her misbehavior became a full time, discouraging job.

Mary Ann's teacher was concerned about her playing by herself.

When other children attempted to play with her, she would become demanding, selfish, unsharing and mean. Her teacher also noted her over-activity and poor attention span. She had great difficulty staying in one place with one activity. She was always in a state of motion. She was easily distracted by any noise or movement of the other children. She grabbed the playthings of her peers without regard for their ownership. She had quick emotional swings from happy to angry to whiny. There were also some noticeable difficulties in her fine motor coordination. She was unable to color within the lines for a child of her age. Of noteworthy importance was that all who knew her said that she would always show remorse and guilt whenever she was scolded. Her teachers and grandparents strongly believed she was a caring and loving child, but her "hyperness" and impulsiveness got in the way of these emotions.

Mary Ann represents many children whose addicted mothers create great difficulties for their offspring. The mother's habitual use and abuse of drugs and alcohol was, most likely, the cause of her daughter's problem behaviors. This condition has been referred to as Attention Deficit Disorder with Hyperactivity. In most instances, it is quite difficult to determine the cause of such a condition. This is largely due to the lack of medical evidence in spite of medical testing.

Attention Deficit Disorder

According to the Diagnostic and Statistical Manual of Mental Disorders,[49] the essential feature of an Attention Deficit Disorder/Hyperactivity Disorder is, "a persistent pattern of inattention and/or hyperactivity-impulsivity that is more frequent and severe than is typically observed in individuals at a comparable level of development."

The following diagnostic criteria for Attention Deficit Disorder/Hyperactivity is inserted to assist the reader in a more detailed comparative understanding of behavior that may co-exist in the *uncaring child*.[50]

A. Either (1) or (2):

(1) Six or more of the following symptoms of **inattention** have persisted for at least six months to a degree that is maladaptive and inconsistent with developmental level:

Inattention

- (a) often fails to give close attention to details or makes careless mistakes in schoolwork, work, or other activities.
- (b) often has difficulty sustaining attention in tasks or play activities.
- (c) often does not seem to listen when spoken to directly.
- (d) often does not follow through on instructions and fails to finish schoolwork, chores, or duties in the workplace (not due to oppositional behavior or failure to understand instructions).
- (e) often has difficulty organizing tasks and activities
- (f) often avoids, dislikes, or is reluctant to engage in tasks that require sustained mental effort (such as schoolwork or home work).
- (g) often loses things necessary for tasks or activities (e.g., toys, school assignments, pencils, books, or tools)
- (h) is often easily distracted by extraneous stimuli.
- (i) is often forgetful in daily activities.

(2) Six or more of the following symptoms of **hyperactivity** impulsivity have persisted for at least six months to a degree that is maladaptive and inconsistent with developmental level:

Hyperactivity

- (a) often fidgets with hands or feet or squirms in seat
- (b) often leaves seat in classroom or in other

situations in which remaining seated is expected.

(c) often runs about or climbs excessively in situations in which it is inappropriate (in adolescents or adults, may be limited to subjective feelings or restlessness)

(d) often has difficulty playing or engaging in leisure activities quitely.

(e) is often "on the go" or often acts as if "driven by a motor"

(f) often talks excessively

Impulsivity

(g) often blurts out answers before questions have been completed.

(h) often has difficulty awaiting turn.

(i) often interrupts or intrudes on other (e.g., butts into conversations or games)

B. Some hyperactive-impulsive or inattentive symptoms that caused impairment were present before age 7 years.

C. Some impairment from the symptoms is present in two or more settings (e.g., at school [or work] and at home).

D. There must be clear evidence of clinically significant impairment in social, academic, or occupational functioning.

E. The symptoms do not occur exclusively during the course of Pervasive Developmental Disorder, Schizophrenia, or other Psychotic disorder and are not better accounted for by another mental disorder (e.g., Mood Disorder, Anxiety Disorder, Associative Disorder, or Personality Disorder).

To determine the presence of ADHD (Attention Deficit/Hyperactivity Disorder), data from the school and family can be most helpful. ADHD cannot be evaluated on the basis of a brief office examination. ADHD doesn't happen suddenly at age six or in the first or fifth grade. Antisocial behavior and/or poor school performance may not be related to ADHD. It may have been caused by other factors such as an emotional disorder or physical illness. The ADHD child's major problem is a physiological one that is caused by heredity, pregnancy influences, birth trauma or circumstance in early childhood. In Mary Ann's situation, we have evidence of a mother's drug and alcohol abuse prior to and during pregnancy. There is problem behavior at birth, i.e., crying at her mother's attempts to breast feed, spitting out her formula, refusal to be held, cuddled or loved and current behavior that describes ADHD. Although Mary Ann's behavior certainly represents the *uncaring* description, her expression of guilt and remorse make it highly unlikely. It is this distinction that separates her from that of the *Uncaring Child Syndrome* and places her into the category of ADHD.

Sean

Sean was a sixteen-year-old teenager whose use and abuse of drugs had been going on for at least a year. From his early childhood, he was described as aggressive and demanding. When he was caught lying and stealing, he would blame others for his deeds. He had little regard for the rights and welfare of others. He rarely, if ever, showed guilt or remorse for what he had done.

By the time Sean was in High School, he was the leader of a gang of his peers. They were known to use drugs, extort money from other school children, bully them and create a basic disturbance to everyone. During the course of his first two years in high school, Sean and his pals served internal and external suspensions. His parents had been called to school on numerous occasions. They admitted they had little control over his attitude and behavior.

On one occasion, Sean was placed in a thirty-day drug rehabilitation facility. He was considered a model client and released to his parents. Within two weeks, he resumed his antisocial behavior. Individual psychotherapy and family counseling was also attempted with no success.

Sean was referred to me by the school counselor who informed me that Sean's parents and the school were unable to stop his destructive behavior. They had assigned him to an alternative classroom, but his negative influence reached out to others whom he led into further disruptions.

As I reviewed Sean's early childhood, parental attitudes and their involvement with him, his response to therapy and drug rehabilitation, a pattern of *uncaring behavior* evolved. First, at the age of two, Sean was demanding, had temper outbursts, was impulsive, defiant and selfish. By the time he was eight, he was known as a bully, liar and antagonizer as well as one who could lead his peers to misbehave. When Sean was in middle school his behavior worsened. He became skilled in conning his teachers and parents. His continual deceptions and lies, without concern for the harm he would do, resulted in frustration, anxiety, anger, and parental guilt.

When Sean was confronted with his misbehavior, he usually blamed his teachers, friends, or family members for his predicament. He rarely took the blame for anything nor did he express guilt or remorse for his wrongdoings.

Sean had an eighteen year old brother and a fourteen year old sister, both of whom did well in school and had the usual number of friends. Neither of them got into any unusual trouble at home or at school. Although there were no serious relationship problems between Sean and his siblings, they could not be considered close.

Sean's experience in individual and family therapy could be described as uneventful. Although his therapist believed he had established a therapeutic relationship with Sean, the counselor was unable to change any of his misbehaviors. Sean's activity in drug rehabilitation was also uneventful. Yet he was considered a model client who caused no problems. Afterwards, however, he did not follow through with a drug or alcohol support group as recommended.

When we look at Sean's behavior during therapy and rehab, we see a young man who "played the system." He knew what was expected from him, and he complied. His conning and sensitivity to know what others wanted was superior. To get what he wanted, he would play the game. What he wanted was to resume his previous pattern of doing *what* he wanted and *when* he wanted.

My approach to Sean's treatment was to first work with the parents in restructuring *their* pattern of behavior. I discussed Sean's dominant personality structure (Chapter 5), and the concept of anxiety, (Chapter 3). I wanted them to have all the ammunition necessary to combat Sean's *uncaring* antisocial behavior. They needed to know that as long as Sean felt no anxiety, he would have no need to make any changes they desired. It was also important for them to know that Sean's behavior could or could not change. They needed to know that even if there was some notable change, he may never become a loving, caring person.

The initial session dealt with educating the parents to the reality of just who Sean was now and who he might become. Although this session was difficult for his parents, they felt a sense of relief knowing they had done all they could in their attempts to help him throughout the years. It was also a relief for them to know......*IT WAS NOT THEIR FAULT!*

During the following session, Sean was confronted with a Six-Step Program (Chapter 7). We outlined the maladaptive behavior targeted for change and the consequences should he not adequately respond. His response was, "that's stupid." During that week, his parents informed me they had no difficulty with Sean at home or at school. I explained the concept of the *"honeymoon period."* The period of quiet before the storm. It was during the second week that the honeymoon ended. Sean was caught lying about homework and was strongly suspected of drug use. His parents quickly enacted Step 4 of the Six Steps, Consequences. They took away his three favorite privileges. Sean immediately attempted to "con" them with denial, lies and promises. When they refused to listen, he had a temper outburst in an attempt to gain control. When he refused to discontinue his tirade, his parents responded by taking away *all* of his privileges for one week. That same night, Sean left home without word. When he didn't"t return home, I instructed the parents to contact the police and file a missing persons report. Two days later, Sean came home. He was in a good mood and acted like nothing had happened. I advised the parents to offer him two choices. One, enter another drug rehab facility with follow up treatment; two, find an alternative place to live. Sean reacted with disbelief, and minimized the episode. His parents held firm in the choices they had offered.

The importance of a highly organized and tightly knit structure cannot be underscored enough. Regaining control and offering limited choices is paramount in dealing with these troublesome children. Sean's choice at this phase could have gone either way. If Sean chose to live elsewhere, he was to be provided adult supervision. A family member could have taken on the task, or the court could have provided supervision. If he chose drug rehab, he was to be closely supervised after his stay terminated. The guidelines presented by the Six-Step Program detailed in Chapter 7 were to be fully implemented. If he failed to comply and continued to be incorrigible, the choice to petition the court would be the alternative.

Sean chose to enter drug rehab. The staff at the rehabilitation facility was more confrontive. The staff recognized his earlier attempts to maintain a facade of compliance. Because Sean was in a tightly structured program, his parents were able to better maintain control over his attempts at manipulation and lying. In family therapy, they made their expectations clear for his return home. They expected him to comply fully with his follow up treatment and to obey rules at home and school. Failure at this level would result in application to the court for its supervision and Sean's placement in a residential setting.

For the first time, Sean took his parents seriously. He knew they would do as they said. He no longer viewed them as merely threatening with no follow through. Although he attempted to con and resist their newly formed pattern of parenting, he did comply. His parents were satisfied with his response although they never felt he was a warm caring or loving son. His antisocial behaviors at school were extinguished as well as his drug and alcohol use. He did however, continue to manipulate his classmates into following his suggestions. He also continued to display many of the above mentioned dominant characteristics. Although, much of the *uncaring behavior* was diminished, it was not gone.

Sean represents the **Operator** as outlined in Chapter 2. His expertise in wheeling, dealing, manipulating combined with his dominant character, and his continual deceptions without concern for others make up a large component of his *uncaring* personality structure. What complicated things more was his drug and alcohol abuse. Without controlling the addiction, it would have been impossible to work on his *uncaring* behaviors.

In many instances Sean's story could have turned out much different. He could have resisted the family, school and rehabilitation attempts to work out the conflict. Had this been the case, Sean's parents would have had to go to court to press for state supervision of Sean. He would have been placed in a residential facility monitored by the state's Children and Youth Services. Once removed from his home, all other choices would be denied him. He would have been forced to comply with the standards, goals, and rules of that facility. His compliance, or lack of compliance, with the rules would have had a direct relationship with the privileges he received. Only when his behavior was deemed improved, for a specified amount of time, would he be considered able to regain his living status with his parents. For many hardcore, resistive *uncaring children*, the removal from their home may be the best alternative.

According to former First Lady, Nancy Reagan,[51] "Drug and alcohol abuse touches all Americans in one form or another, but it is our children who are most vulnerable to its influence. As parents and teachers, we need to educate ourselves about the dangers of drugs so that we can teach our children. And we must go further still by convincing them that drugs are morally wrong."

I don't believe it is enough to teach our children the difference between right or wrong. It is admirable and noble to "Just Say No!" We live in an era when people spend millions of dollars in the education and prevention of drug and alcohol abuse. As drug and alcohol use and abuse is multidimensional, we have enlisted the aid of schools, students, communities and the parents. In many instances, there has been some evidence of success.

Unfortunately, many children are lured into drug abuse by more highly dominant individuals. As more fully detailed in Chapter 5, Follow the Leader, the moderate and lower dominant individuals are more susceptible and more easily influenced by highly dominant individuals. Furthermore, a 1983 *Weekly Reader*[52] survey found that television and movies had the greatest influence on fourth graders in making drugs and alcohol seem attractive; other children had the second greatest influence. From the fifth grade on, peers played an increasingly important role, while television and movies consistently had the second greatest influence. The survey went on to imply the reasons students took drugs. It indicated children needed to "fit," "feel older," and "to have a good time."

Along with the usual preventative means to help our children resist the temptation of drugs and alcohol use and abuse, The *Schools Without Drugs*[53] book cited a number of schools initiating a tough policy for students who were caught possessing or dealing drugs. Although, initiating a tough policy doesn't rid our society of this vile problem, it does however, allow the majority of our children the right to an education without being jeopardized. The most effective school systems utilize the court system in dealing with the users and dealers. Instead of school detention, offenders are hauled off to court. The parents are then notified to assist in the rehabilitation of their children. The child's return to school is contingent upon the cooperation of the parents and the student's successful completion of the prescribed program.

If we are to attempt successful intervention with the *uncaring child*, we must make certain that we can recognize and identify, not only the early soft signs of misbehavior, but the early signs of drug and alcohol use and abuse. Additionally, we must work closely with the school, community and police to help with early prevention. If the *uncaring child* is allowed to escape our detection because of his drug and alcohol use, we are then faced with an even greater obstacle in combating his misconduct.

7

The Treatment Process

"What's done to children they will do to society."

Karl Menninger

Freudian-psychoanalytic theory proposes that the most important events in determining personality structure and psychiatric illness occur during the first seven years of the person's life.[54] Dr. Sigmund Freud believed that each child can be impacted by environment and his biological constitution. He was the first to suggest a special relation-ship between the biology of the individual and his environment. In other words, he felt that a child's psychiatric illness could be caused by both childhood experiences and his own biological makeup.

In the Freudian tradition, the patient is expected to see the analyst four or five times a week for several years. He lies on the couch, is encouraged to say what he wants to a therapist who remains neutral so as not to influence the patient's spontaneous verbal productions. Consequently, the spontaneous verbal productions, called free association, produce patterns of hidden thoughts, conflicts, and insights, which eventually lead to a "cure."

The late Carl Rogers,[55] the "client-centered" therapist, focused on face-to-face therapy rather than the patient lying on the couch. He called people "clients," not patients, so not to demean them as ill. Rogerian therapists are much more active with their clients than Freudian psychoanalysts. Techniques involve restating and summarizing what the client says in an attempt to promote insight and growth, keeping them more focused on their treatment.

During the fifties and sixties, a number of therapists set out to raise the consciousness of society.[56] The human growth movement, as it was called, was expected to give the participants a new experience through feeling, touching and freely expressing their hidden thoughts, anger, ideas and fantasies.

Behavior Modification came of age during the late sixties and early seventies. It was B.F. Skinner,[57] an American psychologist, who first brought the concept of Operant Conditioning into modern focus. Operant (instrumental) conditioning techniques consist of reinforce-ments in the form of rewards, or the withdrawal of punishment when the subject performs a desired behavior. His experiments progressed from laboratory experiments from animals to human beings. Applications of operant techniques in treatment and education have proliferated in recent years.[58]

What follows is a behavioral modification program, with options, designed to be utilized for the *uncaring child*. A case study will be presented later as an example.

During the last thirty years, child rearing methods have virtually remained the same. These methods invariably place a heavy emphasis on the parent to win the cooperation of the child and to be a good listener.[59] Specific techniques such as empathy, genuine regard, and warmth are called reflective responses and are the cornerstones of self-help parenting books and instructional courses. Unfortunately, this material fails to deal effectively with the *uncaring child*, although it often proves helpful for children whose behavior is not as serious.

A detailed, *Six-Step* treatment process is outlined and discussed in this chapter. A comprehensive examination of the child's current behaviors, attitudes, and feelings is clearly delineated for the reader's use. I also provide information about possible roles parents might have adopted in relation to the child. In this way, the parents can identify their own characteristics and respond to their child's manifest behavior. Parents are offered a step-by-step process to both correct the child's maladaptive behavior, and to strengthen their marital relationship and/or support network.

Throughout my thirty-four years of clinical experience, I have been impressed by the volumes of material dealing with parenting issues. I have attended a variety of workshops, parent effectiveness courses, and lectures on the same subject. Unfortunately, the information offered through such sources is incongruent and ineffective in dealing with the *uncaring child*.

This chapter is also intended as a resource for parents, relatives, educators, clinicians, and all others who are in some way involved with an uncaring child. This chapter explains the role of support groups and provides guidelines for selecting an appropriate therapist. Too often, parents spend unnecessary time and money enlisting the aid of therapists who are illequipped to assist them in coping with such children. Instead of helping the family, some therapists may actually exacerbate an already deteriorating situation. I believe the resource information in this chapter will provide help and hope for anyone involved with the *uncaring child*.

The following Treatment Process deals most exclusively with Operant Conditioning techniques.[60]

Step One - Target Behaviors

Make a list of the target problem behaviors -- the behaviors you believe to be disruptive, unhealthy, etc., and arrange them according to their level of importance. For example:

1. lying
2. failing grades
3. chores being ignored or "forgotten"
4. inappropriate anger
5. argumentativeness
6. periodic cursing

7. inattentiveness
8. temper outbursts
9. excessive phone use
10. does not follow the rules
11. bad manners
12. irresponsible
13. rude and insulting
14. bullies and mistreats younger brother or sister
15. mistreats pets
16. teases
17. steals or takes things
18. cheats
19. disobedient and uncooperative
20. drug and alcohol use
21. not coming home
22. runs away
23. physically/verbally abusive

This list will not only highlight the problem behaviors that are disturbing to the household, but it will also serve to develop a therapeutic approach that is simple and free of obstacles.

The following case study will illustrate how the Operant Conditioning Six-Step Program can dramatically improve the behavior of an *uncaring child.*

Mike

Mike came to my office displaying behaviors like those in the Step 1 list. A fourteen-year-old middle child in a family of three children, his parents indicated that he was the only one of their three children evidencing disruptive behavior in the household and at school. They told me he lies about having any homework, in spite of failing grades. He becomes argumentative, angry and uses profanity whenever his parents approach him about his grades and homework. He makes excuses for not doing his chores. His teachers report he does not pay attention to instructions and is usually socializing "too much" with his peers. He rarely helps with the family chores, spending inordinate time at play, watching TV, playing Nintendo or talking on the phone with his friends.

Mike's uncooperativeness has been going on since he was two years old. His parents have had little success gaining his cooperation. Most of their prior attempts to make things better involved talking and appealing to his sense of understanding and fairness to everyone. When this failed, they tried to punish him by grounding. When frustrated by his lack of positive change, they turned to yelling and threats.

The foregoing scenario is quite common in the American family today. The list detailed earlier, attempts to simplify in a logical format the target behaviors that need to be terminated. The parents make this list to simplify what needs to be changed. This list can and should be modified weekly in accordance with the priorities and needs of the parents and the particular behaviors of the child.

Step Two - Privileges and Pleasures

Make a list of the child's pleasures and privileges, (ideally with the child's input) and arrange them in any order. For example:

1. plays with friends
2. Nintendo
3. TV
4. stereo
5. clothes
6. karate lessons
7. use of automobile

8. allowance
9. special food
10. gifts
11. hobbies
12. use of telephone
13. special trips/vacations
14. other pleasures not already mentioned

After making your list of *Privileges and Pleasures,* then arrange them by priority (with the possible assistance of the child), ranging from the activities or possessions they value the most to the one least treasured.

Step Three - Warning!!!

Tell your child that if he/she persists in any of the top three behaviors listed in Step One (*Target Behaviors*), you will restrict them from the list from Step Two (*Privileges and Pleasures),* for a specific length of time. It is of utmost importance that you do not discuss this issue at length and do not attempt to use it as a fear tactic or to instill guilt. Also, avoid expressing anger and punitive statements. The manner in which you approach your child should be non-threatening and casual.

Step Four - Consequences

When you learn of any violations from Step One, (*Target Behaviors*) swiftly, in a calm but firm manner, restrict the top three in Step Two *(Privileges and Pleasures).* The length of time you remove your child's privileges depends on the degree of violations. This generally runs from three to six hours to one day to one week. Conceivably, it could be longer for more serious conditions. If your child's behavior persists during the time of his restriction or additional conflicts arise from your attempts to rectify his misbehavior, all privileges from Step Two *(Privileges and Pleasures)* should be restricted. During the time of his penalty, do not engage in any discussion of his dilemma or any issue that may be related. This discussion must only take place at the penalty's conclusion. Discussions with the child during the penalty phase will only contaminate the effect of the consequence. In fact, if he persists in discussing his dilemma, tell him that you will not discuss it until the termination of his penalty, and if he brings it up again, the penalty will become longer, and the remaining privileges (from the Step 2 *Privileges and Pleasures)* will be terminated. Remember, your child is the master of deception, and if there was a college degree for this type of behavior, he would most certainly receive a Ph.D.

Step Five - Overcorrection

Frequently, taking away *Privileges and Pleasures* is not enough to get your message across. Sometimes we have to take more drastic steps to gain their attention and cause them sufficient anxiety to make the necessary change. Over-correction is the use of multiple consequences when a lack of compliance occurs. For example, if your child fails to comply, in spite of taking away all of his *Privileges and Pleasures, Over-correction* is enforced in the following manner: You simply add a long list of chores that your child must complete before he can be considered for normal *Privileges and Pleasures*. For example, you might say to your child, "While you are grounded for the next week, you will not have the privilege of watching TV, listening to your stereo, using the telephone, leaving the house, or having any of your friends visit, etc., AND you will also be expected to perform three or more of the following before privileges are reinstated.

1. clean your room
2. clean the bathroom
3. wash the car
4. wash the dishes
5. vacuum the carpet

6. dust
7. wax floors
8. other chores you can think of

Step Six - Reward

When you believe your child is responding positively to the consequence of his behavior -- when there is positive change -- it is essential that you reward him with a hug, pat on the back, and a few positive remarks. But - **Do Not Overdo Your PRAISE.** You can then reinstate all of his privileges from Step 2 (*Privileges and Pleasures*).

When Mike was presented with the discussion as outlined in Step 3 *(Warning)*, he said, "This is stupid." After his attempts to impede his parents intervention failed, Mike settled down and complied. One and a half weeks later, one of Mike's teachers informed his parents that he was not doing his homework and was failing. When Mike was approached by his parents, he became angry, cursed and stomped out of the house. When he returned, his parents repeated Step Three *(Warning)*. During that week, Mike's parents caught him in several lies and determined he was not doing homework and "forgetting" to do his agreed upon chores. Additionally, he sulked and was belligerent. Mike was told all of his privileges were being restricted until his three target problem behaviors in Step One *(Target Behaviors)* were resolved.

Of special importance to parents: It is up to you to determine how many target problem behaviors should be considered for elimination. It is my belief, when you are faced with continued resistance and defiance of fair expectations, you have the right to eliminate *all* pleasures and privileges until you have the child's full compliance.

The weeks that followed were difficult. Mike's parents faced anxiety and guilt for restricting their son's "normal existence." At times they talked about reinstating some of his privileges in spite of his non-compliance. They were on the phone with me at least four times a week for support.

Several weeks later, Mike made his drastic change. He began

bringing home books, stopped swearing and lying. Teachers indicated a general improvement in his grades and attitude. Mike's parents enacted Step Six *(Reward)* and reinstated all his privileges.

Mike slipped several times throughout the year. He periodically needed reminders, Step Four *(Consequences)* to bring him back to compliance. Joyfully, his parents remarked, "We now have a son and a future."

In observing the success in Mike's treatment process, we must not look towards his experiencing guilt or remorse for his misbehaviors. If we are to be successful, we must produce anxiety or dread. Anxiety is never wanted or wished for. Mike certainly didn't look forward to losing his privileges. When he discovered his parents couldn't be intimidated nor manipulated, he only had two choices. One, to continue to be without, or two, comply and make certain concessions granting him his lost privileges. Mike chose to keep his privileges and comply with his parents' expectations. But they were fortunate. Many parents of *uncaring children* refuse to buy into their parents needs and expectations regardless of how fair they may be. In Mike's case, he has graduated from high school and is currently in community college. Although Mike and his parents continue to have difficulties in their relationship, his parents feel a sense of relief that he has activated healthy behavior in setting healthy and meaningful future goals.

The Six-Step program is designed to help parents respond effectively to tumultuous disruptive behavior. This is an effective and powerful system that simplifies parent/child conflicts.

SPECIAL CONSIDERATION

Remarriage:

During the eighties and into the nineties, there has been an increase in the number of remarried families. With remarriage comes the problems of family roles. Who is who in this newly blended family? Children often resent "the intruder," the nonbiological parent, and soon designate him or her as the villain. They often feel displaced in their traditional roles and feel threatened when change is suggested. At the same time, natural parents feel a special alliance to their own children and may easily be manipulated by a child who wants to be rescued from the stepparent. The parents soon begin to battle, and the wedge between the marriage partners widens as greater turmoil erupts within the entire family. This allows the child to escape his responsibility while pitting one parent against the other.

In spite of earlier psychological teachings insisting that parents speak from one voice and maintain a mutuality when it comes to the children, my experience with remarried families having to deal with *uncaring children* does not fit this traditional mold. My advice to the remarried parents of an *uncaring child* is that they accept different roles when it comes to discipline. The natural parent must be the one who manages the discipline. This way, there is no contamination of purpose or dividing of parental loyalties. It avoids creating any major problems before they become a source of even more problems. *We want to avoid parental bickering over issues unrelated to the child's behavior. We must therefore insure that the non-biological parent be removed as the one responsible for expanding the current crisis.* The non-biological parent will only complicate an already difficult situation.

Natural Parents:

Contrary to the advice I gave to remarried parents, I suggest strongly that natural parents work together and take a mutual position when it comes to dealing with the rearing of their children. Unlike with remarried parents, the child of natural parents has a much clearer perception of the roles within the family. Unless we are dealing with dysfunctional parents, the child's role has not become jeopardized by the "intrusion" of a new surrogate parent. His parents are the same people that have been there from the beginning. It is this concept that connects and distinguishes them from the remarried couple. Therefore, they must join and demonstrate a mutual understanding, as well as authority, for the child to model.

Single Parents:

Prior to 1945 everyone knew what a mother and father was "supposed" to do. Children had their roles in going to school and assisting with family chores. Then came the 50's, a freer time without a depression or world war. The fifties represented a more happy time in America for the family. The music and the dancing was fun. The kids had neighborhoods and playmates. There was a feeling of family togetherness. The sixties ushered in the Vietnam war, drugs, free sex, and the beginning of the end of the traditional family. The family relocated for financial reasons and to live in a more desirable surrounding. Mothers were now in careers and helping with the family finances. The family began counting on two salaries to exist. As the roles became more uncertain and stressful, career stress increased and the nations' economic status worsened, divorce increased dramatically. As the divorce rate increased, its effect on the American child became more noticeable. Not only do the parents experience the crisis, but so do the children. Single parents experienced financial decline, emotional and physical void, depression, anger and rage, agitation, and fear of their children's emotional harm.

Many parents come to me asking, "Would our children do better if we stayed together until they are grown?" In my experience, the majority of children from broken homes tell me they would have preferred their parents remaining together, rather than divorcing. They feel their lives were "ruined" due to divorce.

Children disapprove of any change in their environment. When change of the magnitude of divorce occurs, the family structure is often traumatized. Failing grades, depression, anxiety, and anger result when children are subjected to the disillusionment of their parents marriage. Therefore, it is extremely important to empower these children with the customary roles previously performed. *In other words, don't usurp or change the child's duties or responsibilities because of change in mates.*

When single parents are faced with disciplining an *uncaring child*, the task is complicated by guilt. A single mother, for instance, attempts to offset any perceived emotional harm caused by the divorce. If she feels her child is in danger of experiencing anxiety or depression, she tends to rescue her child from the pain. Therefore, the single parent will back away from making the child face the consequences for his misbehavior. Both parents blamethe other for the child's problems and the child escapes responsibility for his actions.

Unmotivated Children:

Applications of operant techniques in treatment and education have become increasingly important. Tokens or poker chips have been used effectively with children as young as 2 1/2 to early adolescence. The Token Economy has been particularly popular.[61] The reason for its popularity is that it is a powerful tool that brings forth desired behavior.

In a Token Economy the child is paid by tokens, points or other means of specially designed currency, (not money) for completion of various academic tasks and for select social behaviors. It is important to choose an appropriate token that can not be reproduced or copied by the child. The tokens can purchase a number of things including special foods, room furnishings, and clothing. Tokens or Poker chips can be purchased in different sizes and colors. If you are working with more than one child in the family, each color or size can be assigned to each child.

In order for the Token Economy to work, it must have several pre-requisites. The target behaviors need to be identified, a procedure for reward must be developed and procedures to deal with the maladaptive behavior must be in place. In some cases, there are children who appear not to care if their privileges are removed. They take a stance of defiance and demonstrate no perceived response from the parents' best efforts. This type of non-responsive behavior on the part of the child results in the parent feeling hopeless and hapless.

Token reinforcers seem to help motivate some children who otherwise would just prefer to be grounded and without pleasure. They have been of extreme usefulness in working with antisocial and delinquent youths who have committed serious offenses.[62] The Token Reinforcer can be applied to the youth whose behavioral patterns (e.g., failing grades, truancy, running away, and other misbehaviors) may lead to further decline.

Many parents who face a *uncaring child,* resort to a variety of coping responses which do not help to change the undesired behavior. One is to pay the child for performing specified tasks. This is known as a one-to-one ratio. When the child is paid directly for a prescribed behavior, i.e., washing the car, mowing the lawn, etc., he takes the money and runs, unmotivated to discontinue undesirable behaviors. When he is given tokens however, he must wait until he has produced enough tokens for his reward. This could be a five or ten to one ratio. There is a greater predictability in extinguishing maladaptive behavior using token reinforcers than by paying him directly for the completion of a given task. Of special note is to insure that the reward is sufficient incentive to encourage desirable behavior. For example, a child will not be interested in working for something that does not appeal to him.

Untreatables (Treatment Resistors):

Unfortunately, there are those children who fall into the category of "treatment resistant" or untreatables. Children of this ilk seem to lack the ability to learn from their experience and continue to repeat behaviors that get them into trouble with their parents, school and law enforcement authorities. These are the same children that are sent to juvenile detention, time and time again, without discontinuing the *uncaring* behavior that initially placed them there. No matter what consequences they are forced to endure, they fail to learn from their mistakes and continue to repeat patterns of *uncaring* and unhealthy behaviors. In my clinical experience, about one out of twenty (5%) fall into the category that can be labeled, "treatment resistors."

REVIEW OF THE TREATMENT PROCESS

Let us now review the actual treatment process and its ramifications. The Six-Step program, although seeming rather simplistic, is a process that is uncomfortable for parents. To deprive our children of their pleasures, may for the most part, seem uncomplicated; however, it can create insurmountable guilt and anxiety in some of us. We become more interested in insuring our children's relief from pain and suffering. We believe that if our children are too unhappy, we are failing as parents. We therefore fail to teach the child impulse control guidelines.

Parent/Child Reaction:

Let us, for a moment, examine the child's and parent's reaction to the Six-Steps. The child's initial reaction may be to mock the parents' attempts at correcting their behavior. They may even fool you by behaving properly. This, however, lasts for only a short time; they will quickly revert to their usual disruptive pattern of behavior.

Parents must be extremely careful at this point. In their roles as "good and loving" parents, they want so much for their child to behave well, that they will often reward the child, prematurely, for any positive sign. Parents are also fearful of losing the love of their children if they are perceived as being unfair and harmful.

As stated in Chapter Three, anxiety must be present if change is to occur. If your child experiences no anxiety, you will probably not observe any meaningful and lasting change. Anxiety will only occur when you, the parent, create sufficient turmoil in the child's world by maintaining strict, consistent action in the form of discipline. This action may precipitate his crisis, but this is the prescription for change. Remember, this is your child's crisis, not yours. *It is imperative that you no longer maintain your belief that this is your problem. This is your child's problem and his/her crisis.*

When parents attempt to correct their child's disruptive behavior, they experience a great deal of anxiety because of their involvement and concern for their child's well being and their genuine feelings of love. On the other hand, the *uncaring child* is concerned only with his/her own well being and comfort. As long as he/she is able to maintain this level of serenity, without interruption, he/she will exhibit few problems, but will make little change. It is only when expectations are presented to the child that we quickly see evidence of *uncaring behaviors*.

Pat

Let us examine Pat's attitudes, feelings, and behaviors. He fits into the role of the "transformer," basically "normal" with few problems in growing up. He was the child, for all intents and purposes, who was the "good boy" from the beginning. His problems didn't begin until about age twelve, when he began to follow the lead of his more dominant peers. He was easily led by the stronger, more aggressive and dominant males in his peer group. As the quieting pubescence ended and the yearnings of adolescence approached, Pat began to explore independence. Unfortunately, following the more dominant peers in his group resulted in antisocial behaviors.

During individual psychotherapy Pat was pleasant and agreeable to work with during individual psychotherapy. Initially, he appeared interested in working out his problems; however, when no progress was made, he became negative. When he was asked, "What seems to be the problem?" his response was, "I have no problem; my parents do. They overreact to everything and get on my case."

Traditional psychotherapeutic techniques had little effect, and attempts to establish a working therapeutic relationship failed. Regardless of how well the relationship between Pat and me progressed, his behavior at home and school remained unchanged.

When Pat's parents began the Six-Step approach, they experienced some difficulty during the first two weeks. Although they appeared motivated and enthusiastic, they reported being negligent in their efforts to comply with Step Four (*Consequences*). They were too quick to let Pat "off the hook" when they perceived his positive response. Obviously, Pat was able to "con" his parents into believing he was going to do as they expected. In reality, he was able to forestall his punishment.

After his parents applied Step Four in a more consistent manner, Pat reacted with anger, and attempted to discuss with his mother the *why's* and *how come's* of their reaction to his "normal" behaviors. They removed all the items in Step Two (*Privileges and Pleasures*) and made his penalty longer due to his continued discussion and misconduct.

After several weeks of both improving and failing, they began to see a steady improvement in his overall attitude and productivity at home and at school. He quickly verbalized his unwillingness to continue to lose privileges. His parents viewed his progress as a "miracle."

Winnie

Winnie was a fifteen-year-old, only child. Her occasional use of drugs and alcohol, lying, petty stealing, and disobedient behavior brought her to the attention of the police, school counselor, State Welfare Office, and a family therapist. Though she received counseling at home and school, she continued to be a problem at home and school. Her parents and her school counselor were unable to gain her cooperation. Traditional individual and family psychotherapy was attempted, but failed.

From an early age, Winnie was considered spoiled and easily irritated. She had little interest in playing by herself and was easily bored. She constantly sought her parents' attention, and when they attempted to redirect her, she threw temper tantrums. They had problems getting her to do homework; her grades were average. At age eleven, her grades fluctuated between D's and F's. By the time she was thirteen, she had lost all interest in her school work and was failing.

This picture is fairly common among *uncaring children*. There were many early soft signs with Winnie that the parents were untrained to observe. They were truly caring and loving parents, but they felt the usual guilt and frustration experienced by such "good" parents. I believe these parents could have been successful much earlier had they had applied the Six-Step program.

When Winnie was brought to my attention, she behaved in much the same way she had with her previous therapists. After trying the traditional approach without success, I suggested that the parents apply the Six-Step program. The target problem behaviors were as follows:

Step One (Target Behaviors)

1. drugs/alcohol
2. stealing
3. lying
4. disobedience
5. failing grades
6. temper tantrums

Step Two *(Privileges and Pleasures)*

1. socializing with friends
2. telephone
3. TV
4. either buying clothes or shopping

To the parents' surprise, Winnie's response was positive. During the first two weeks, her previous misbehavior ceased. I reminded them of the "honeymoon" period - the initial reaction that appears positive, but is quickly interrupted by misbehavior. After two weeks, Winnie became belligerent and defiant. They quickly reacted to her regression and imposed Step Four *(Consequences)*. Winnie's response was to leave home. Her parents were depressed and guilt-ridden. They felt that they might have been "too hard" on her and that she might do something foolish. After much reassurance, they contacted the police and reported her missing.

Winnie's running away from home and the subsequent parental guilt is not uncommon at this phase of intervention. The *uncaring child* may react to parental control by renewing and increasing her parent's anxiety and guilt.

In a situation like Winnie's, parents must reinstate the original Six-Step program upon her return. If she continues to oppose her parents with dangerous behaviors, Step Four *(Over-correction)* should be enacted. The adolescent should be told that she must perform a number of chores while she is being denied her usual privileges. Go along with the process, or remain grounded. If positive results do not follow disciplinary action, the alternative is to place her in an alternative living arrangement. This could range from short-term psychiatric placement to long-term residential care for behavioral disorders.

In this case, Winnie was brought home by the police. Her parents gave her choices. She could comply with house rules, or choose to live in a State approved residence. After explaining her alternatives, Winnie chose to comply. Although she attempted to argue and make her parents feel guilty for being so "uptight," Winnie finally settled down and did what was expected of her.

In the summary above, it is easy to see how parents can be manipulated and compelled to end punitive actions. We must look at Winnie's running away as her reaction to her parent's mandates. If she felt she could confuse and obstruct her parent's actions, she thought she could return to previous antisocial behaviors without fear of any consequences. Parents must be diligent and consistent in their discipline if *uncaring* behavior is to be remediated.

Choosing A Therapist:

I have alluded to the difficulty psychotherapists have in dealing effectively with the *uncaring child*. Choosing an appropriate therapist is a difficult but mandatory task. The therapist must have not only the traditional training skills required of a clinician, but the added knowledge, required skills, and a genuine understanding of the "good parents" dilemma. As previously stated, too often the therapist looks for the faults of the parents and can easily miss the masked *Uncaring Child Syndrome*. The therapist may then turn his tactics to family therapy which has repeatedly failed. This same pattern of failed attempts to resolve conflicts continues, resulting in more frustration, guilt and suffering.

The following is a suggested list of mandatory skills needed by the psychotherapist in order to recognize, identify and work with the *uncaring child*:

1. Sound knowledge of psychosocial development. The therapist should be thoroughly trained in the various forces that mold human personality.

2. Experience in traditional parenting techniques: i.e. Parent Effectiveness Training (PET) and Systematic Training for Effective Parenting (STEP). This experience is helpful in delineating the *uncaring child* from the non-uncaring child.

3. Marriage and family therapy skills for the purpose of understanding functional and dysfunctional family systems.

4. Sound knowledge of behavioral therapy techniques.

5. Clear understanding of normal and abnormal child development.

6. Empathetic understanding of the family turmoil and the ability to know the difference between "bad" parents with "good" children and "good" parents with "bad" children.

Those characteristics, as well as traditional knowledge and skills, are a prerequisite when choosing a psycho-therapist to intervene with your family. Obviously, because of the lack of therapists trained with the sensitivity and understanding of the *uncaring child* concept, the question arises: Where do we find such a therapist?

Through my practice in South and Central Florida, I have found a helpful source for finding the appropriate therapist through Toughlove.[63] They are a self-help program with more than 800 groups throughout the United States and Canada for parents troubled with their childrens' behavior. The Toughlove groups, with which I am acquainted, are sympathetic to parents and the problems associated with unsuccessful therapeutic interventions, excessive financial and emotional cost, and the tragic consequences of a fractured family. They have had much experience with the "traditional psychotherapist" and have been disillusioned by the lack of positive results. Therefore, they have developed their own referral network of agencies, therapists, attorneys, treatment facilities, etc., especially sensitive to their dilemma.

Other support groups that might be considered are P.E.T.[64] and S.T.E.P.[65] These programs are recommended to help understand normal and problem behavior.

8

Ask The Doctor

"Children today love luxury. They have bad manners, a contempt for authority, a disrespect for their elders and they like to talk instead of work. They contradict their parents, chatter before company, gobble up the best at the table, and tyrannize over their teachers."

Socrates - 500 B.C. - Athens.

As with any method that deals with unfamiliar territory, many questions arise from its exploration. I will attempt to answer these questions as frankly and candidly as possible. I am also aware that any answer to complicated issues may be incomplete, lacking the full dimension of the particular issues presented. I will make every effort to respond with that in mind and to suggest further investigation through other sources and literature.

Ask The Doctor

1. What causes the Uncaring Child Syndrome?

I believe it is constitutional. In other words, it involves inherited elements that are transmitted to the child. I believe these kids have a predisposition to certain behaviors and personality traits.

Some evidence suggests the XYY syndrome (a genetic disorder in which individuals possess an extra male chromosome) produces a genetic predisposition for crime. These individuals may not commit violent crimes, but they do tend to commit minor offenses.[66]

When there are several children in the family and only one turns out "bad," how do we explain the remaining members' positive outcomes? In spite of the parents' repeated attempts to work these conflicts out, the *uncaring child* remains unchanged. We just cant write it off as a result of his position in the family -- youngest, middle, oldest. Neither can we continuc to blame the parents, especially when there is evidence that they are blameless. This is not to say, however, that no evidence suggest that certain parents cause messed up kids. I have seen many kids who have come from uncaring and abusive parents. The results of bad parenting are well documented. This is not the case, however, with *"good parents"* raising unresponsive, *"bad children."* It is about time we look more closely at these children and place the burden on them when appropriate.

2. What are the earliest signs of the syndrome?

Early warning signs are offered in Chapter Four as soft signs. The earliest ones can be seen at about the age of two to two-and-a-half. The complaints heard most often are: "He doesn't listen to me. She rarely finishes what she begins. He is easily distracted by noises or people. She has difficulty keeping her mind on what she is doing. He's impulsive. I can't turn my back on her. He has no patience. She fidgets. He can't play alone. She's hyper, gets upset and displays her temper if things don't go her way. He's disobedient. She has little or no regard for the rights of others. He's oppositional, easily upset, accident prone, demanding, manipulative, and defiant. She has sudden mood swings, expects others to indulge her, takes unnecessary risks, blames others, denies wrongdoing, and seeks the forbidden. He has the knack for forgetfulness. She holds contempt for advice."

It continues to amaze me that a child so young has the ingredients of so many characteristics of an older child. Because of this, I advise parents to look at these soft signs as red flags -- early warning signs that alert us to potential problems. If we can be alerted early enough, we may reverse certain undesirable behavior before it becomes more severe or irreversible.

3. Are their any soft signs for the infant or toddler?

In some more advanced children, we may see some of the soft signs at an earlier age; however, it is not until about the age of two to two-and-a-half that we begin to see a more consistent pattern. Also, prior to that age, their behavior is at the exploratory level, and trying to identify soft signs would be confusing and probably meaningless.

4. I am the mother of a six-year-old boy. He has had behavioral problems since he was two. My pediatrician told me, "He will grow out of it." What do you think?

Ever since I can remember, pediatricians, professional counselors, and other advice-giving professionals have been saying to parents, "They will grow out of it," for a variety of complaints about behavior. I believe, however, we should look at any behavior that concerns us if it persists for more than two week. I do not believe problem behavior merely disappears by children "growing out of it." My experience has been just the contrary. Behaviors that persist for more that two weeks in spite of attempts to change them have developed into other more serious behaviors. For example, a child who lies about doing homework might at some point begin lying about his whereabouts, drinking & stealing.

5. Do you find any specific physical medial problems with the Uncaring Child?

On the contrary, I have rarely been able to associate any medical problems with UCS. These children seem to be in good physical health, both medically and neurologically.

6. Do children who are labeled with Attention Deficit Hyperactivity also possess characteristics of UCS?

I do find that many children with the label of Attention Deficit Hyperactivity Disorder have similarities to *uncaring children* in their early behavior. They may exhibit inattention, restless movement, distractibility, poor concentration, hyperactivity, and impulsivity. However, their capacity to feel subjective anxiety separates them from the *uncaring child*. Therefore, I do not see a relationship between those children who have ADHD with those who have UCS, unless they have characteristics of both.

To illustrate this point further, let us look at the following portrait. Billy is an eight-year-old who has problems finishing things he starts. He has trouble listening, concentrating, playing by himself, and organizing his school work. He is hyperactive and he is beginning to lie about doing his homework.

When Billy's school counselor suggested that he might have ADHD, a specialized program at school was initiated. As the problems associated with ADHD were being attended to, at home and at school, his lying behavior stopped. Billy's parents remarked that they always believed he felt guilt and remorse for his lying.

The above picture is always different when dealing with the *uncaring child*. If Billy were an *uncaring child*, we would see a host of other misbehaviors associated with the syndrome -- blaming others, defiance, selfishness, lack of learning from experience, lack of guilt or remorse, unresponsive to parents, etc.. His response would also be negative to almost all attempts to correct his behavior.

7. What do the Uncaring Children become when they are adults?

When an *uncaring child* begins to pursue antisocial behavior, it is remarkable how rarely they will change course. The adult *uncaring child* is poorly equipped to deal with responsibilities of a male/female relationship, let alone rearing children. They are unable to be intimate in relationships although they may give the appearance of intimacy to their observers. Much like the Borderline Personality Disorder,[67] they may be impulsive or unpredictable, unstable and intense in their interpersonal relationships, or demonstrate intense anger or lack of control. They could be emotionally unstable, with shifts in mood; and may have bolts of suicidal or homicidal ideas or gestures. Just as they are unable to adopt healthy standards, goals, values, or ideals, they are almost impotent in developing empathy, genuineness, warmth, or respect in intimate relationships.

Some of these individuals will actually appear to be making improvements in their lives by adopting newly formed roles, which may come in several forms, such as religious conversion or job status; however, they will maintain their *uncaring* pursuits.

8. I am the parent of a fifteen-year-old girl. She refuses to listen to me. She's failing all of her subjects at school; she's disrespectful, and I believe she is using drugs. I have tried cutting off all of her privileges, but now she sneaks out of the house late at night. I have received calls from the school about her lack of attendance. We tried counseling, but that was a joke. Nothing we have tried has worked. What can I do?

The first thing you have to ask yourself is, "How far am I willing to go?" Although it is impossible for me to know clearly if she is an *uncaring child*, the treatment suggested is much the same as it would be for any child with extreme behavior. Would you be willing to put your child in a residential facility for an undetermined length of time? If you merely use this step as a threat, and have no intention to proceed, your child quickly sees it as an invitation to further her antisocial behavior.

Let us suppose you have followed the treatment program as outlined in Chapter 6. If your child's misbehavior continued, I would recommend she be placed in a residential facility, not only to control her misbehavior, but to prevent any harm coming to her or others.

Should that be the case, you could calmly tell your child that you are in the process of locating a residential placement for her and then do it. If she is willing to work on changing the misbehaviors (as outlined in Chapter 6), then residential placement could be dropped.

9. How can you get children to understand that they are responsible for their own behavior?

It is essential for you to create the perception that it

is your child's choice to either continue misbehavior or to terminate it. Also, they must know that it is their choice whether or not they gain or lose privileges. This takes away the perception of it being the parents' fault. Remember, it is the anxiety of the child that will eventually make them desire change. The parents <u>must</u> initiate/produce anxiety in the child because the child does not feel any anxiety beyond the moment. Always place the responsibility of his behavior on him.

10. How do you deal with a child who does not care if you take her privileges away? She seems to lack any concern about being grounded or any other restrictions.

Every so often, I see a child who "takes on the family," or appears ambivalent. It is a battle of nerves fought by the child's passive/aggressivity. In this battle, however, the child accepts her parents' response to her behavior, and instead of making any attempt to regain her privileges, she concedes to the punishment. The child's passive response leads to utter frustration by the parents. They feel hopeless and angered by the child's passive restraint and lack of concern.

After you strip the child of all privileges and she appears to have accepted total grounding, make a list of household chores for her to complete. The completion of each chore would grant her a home-bound privileges only. She is not to have any out-of-home privileges until all the chores have been satisfied. In this way, we attempt to regain her cooperation by meaningful activity.

11. I have a twenty-year-old son who has had a behavior problem most of his life. He has always beenunreliable and untruthful. He is an alcoholic, sober for two weeks. Between therapists and rehabilitation programs I have spent a fortune on his recovery. The longest he has been sober is three months. He says he is working and

needs a car and insurance so he can maintain his job. I have always helped him in the past but have felt manipulated. I am afraid not to help him now. What should I do?

This appears to be a case of co-dependency. Your continued efforts to help your son is, in actuality, a rescue mission. The responsibility of sobriety is his, not yours. You must first make known your limits and expectations if you are going to assist him. First, he must be in an Alcoholics Anonymous program. If necessary, he should be in an alcohol rehabilitation program. He must then maintain sobriety for six months before you consider assisting him further.

It is essential that you no longer provide any financial support to him without his sobriety and participation in AA for a period of six months. This places the full responsibility of his recovery on him, not you. The only measure of his recovery is on what he does, not what he says. When he has fulfilled your expectations, you may trust in his word, at least for this particular episode. After the six month period of his consistent participation in his recovery, you can then assist him with support. But be careful you do not sabotage it by another emotional and financial rescue. Go slow and easy in your giving. Remember, you have been the sucker before, and it is easy to rekindle the past co-dependent behavior.

Discontinue feeding the fire of illness and feed only the momentum of success. Your attempts to rescue and provide for your child serve only to allow him to continue feeding off you without giving back. Parasitic taking is common with not only the addictive personality, but also with the *uncaring child.*

12. What do you mean when you refer to a "bad" parent?

When I talk about bad parents, I mean the parents that are typically described by psychotherapists as causing problems in their children through their own inadequacies or harmful behavior. They may be rejecting, abusive, deviant, or traumatizing. This does not mean, however, that these parents are unable to change their "bad" behavior. With the help of family therapy, and the proper motivation, the outcome may be positive.

13. *I am afraid if I take discipline too far with my daughter, she will run away, use drugs or take up with sleazy characters.*

First of all, we must evaluate the toll uncaring behavior takes. It disturbs the lives of those involved with the *uncaring child*. If this behavior goes unchecked, the results can be devastating. In spite of your fears of losing your child to the street, you must take charge while attempting to redirect her misdirected, destructive energy. If the child chooses to go on the street, we must choose options to meet the crisis. These options may include the police or children and youth protective services. You must not be intimidated or threatened by your child's fleeing. You must take a stand, knowing that you are doing the best you can, considering the circumstances.

14. *My teenage son has been punching and kicking holes in the wall when he gets mad. He is verbally abusive, makes threats to leave home, and blames us for his unhappiness. What do you suggest we do?*

The first thing I would recommend is to contact a family therapist who has a clear understanding of behavioral therapy and family system skills. The therapist could determine the presence of an emotional illness or the formation of symptoms that may account for his behavior. If this intervention fails to uncover, mediate, and resolve his behavior, I would then review and implement the Six-Step approach as outlined in Chapter 7. If he is not evidencing any symptoms of depression, the Six-Step approach may be extremely useful in extinguishing his maladaptive behavior.

15. *Should I take my sixteen-year-old daughter's threat of killing herself seriously? She has made this threat on two other occasions, but has never done anything about it.*

Yes! Absolutely! Most suicidal individuals will be suicidal for a brief period. When suicidal individuals contemplate suicide, they are feeling worse than they have ever before and they want to stop that horrible pain at any cost. It is essential that you take a suicidal threat seriously. You daughter's verbal warning indicates a serious threat and should not be taken casually.

16. *My boy is four years old. Is he too young for me to begin working on his temper outbursts?*

Definitely not. I believe you can work on changing misbehavior as early as children are able to understand you. When a child begins to explore areas of the house that might be dangerous, it is important to draw safe and dangerous boundaries. If you stop a child from putting his hand on a hot stove, you are teaching him the same principal. More generally, you should be teaching the child ideals, standards, and goals during his entire early development. A temper tantrum is socially unacceptable, as it infringes on the rights of others. Work on changing this behavior as soon as possible.

17. *I am the parent of three children. The middle child*

is making us crazy by refusing to do chores, leaving his room a mess, lying, and constantly having school problems. He seems unconcerned with our feelings and I am convinced he takes no responsibility for any of his actions. My other two children are fine and cause few problems. My concern is that I am spending most of my time with the middle child and feel I am neglecting the others. Also, I don't know if I am doing more harm than good. My husband and I are either spending hours talking to him or grounding him. We are feeling guilt, frustration, and anger. We no longer know what is right. Please help!

My first advice would be to find a family therapist skilled in behavioral therapy and family systems skills. Family issues that may be creating the problem need to be explored and worked through. It is also important for the rest of the family to have a realistic view of what your child's behavior is doing to each person individually and to the family as a whole. Allow him, and the rest of the family, to take responsibility for their choices, making the consequences of their choices clear. If other family members help reinforce the Six-Step program it will probably be easier to live through. As parents of a misbehaving and possibly *uncaring child*, you must deal with him in a relaxed, guiltless manner. His defiant, selfish, and indifferent attitude makes him almost impossible to reach. Guilt, therefore, is a waste of time and energy. I would stop talking about gaining his cooperation and attempt to make him feel guilt or remorse for his actions. This is the time to act, not to talk. Allow him to experience the consequences of his choices, regardless of how long it takes. If he chooses to disregard your expectations, act on the consequences as discussed in Chapter 7.

18. I am the mother of a thirteen-year-old girl who has been a behavioral problem since my remarriage two years ago. My husband insists that she is spoiled and that I am inconsistent in my parenting. He is always on her case for chores, homework, and petty behavior. I am worried that my marriage may break up if this continues. What should I do?

This appears to be a common problem in the world of remarriage. Since the eighties, and now in the nineties, the divorce rate has spiraled upwards. Previously, parents were told to, "Act as one voice. Be mutual in your discipline. Do not allow the child to get between you and your spouse."

Although this is still good advice for natural parents, it is not very sound for those who have remarried. Because of the disruption to the family's stability and established roles, the new member must resist changing that structure.

Remember, this family existed before the new member's arrival. The new member must not join or overshadow his or her spouse when it comes to parenting issues. The only time I advise new members of remarried families to intervene is when the behavior of the children interferes directly with his or her personal life. For example, if a child uses his stepfather's tools without permission, the stepfather has the right to discuss this with the child. However, any disciplinary actions should be discussed by both parents and then the natural parent should deal with the discipline. Children may resent a new member's dominant role which may make them feel misplaced and displaced.

19. I have gotten calls from the school to inform me of my twelve-year-old son's terrible behavior. They say he is disrupting the class by his interruptions, noises, and

general cutting up. He has difficulty finishing his work and may fail most of his subjects. He is not a big problem at home, but he does tease his seven-year-old sister too much. What help can you offer?

Several things need to be looked at in order to properly understand the roots of this problem. First, we must determine the possibility of a learning disorder and/or attention deficit, with or without hyperactivity. This can usually be accomplished by psychological testing at school. He may be covering up his weakness by misbehavior. Secondly, I would handle the teasing behavior by using the Six-Step program as outlined in Chapter 7. The following summary may be helpful:

Step 1. **(Target Behavior)**
Target behavior is teasing.

Step 2 **(Privileges and Pleasures)**
List his privileges and pleasurable activities.

Step 3 **(Warning)**
Inform child of consequence if behavior persists.

Step 4 **(Consequence)**
Removal of three favorite privileges from Step 2

Step 5 **(Over-correction)**
Additional chores while being grounded if condition does not improve

Step 6 **(Reward)**
Reward for not teasing

20. *My sixteen-year-old son admittedly smokes marijuana. He says this drug is safe and will do no harm. He is managing to do average school work and is not creating any serious problems at home. I am still concerned about him and fear the worst. I am afraid if I try to ground him or punish him, he will leave home and live on the street.*

Ask The Doctor

There are several problems associated with your son's behavior. First, marijuana is illegal. He is breaking the law by smoking the drug. Second, there is a downside after any amount of use. It includes decreased eye-hand coordination, making driving and other mechanical operations unsafe. There is evidence that the use of marijuana can cause problems with respiratory, endocrine, and immune systems. There is more risk of cancer due to marijuana than with cigarettes. Also, in spite of ill informed claims to the contrary, marijuana is addicting.

If you need further indication that marijuana is injurious to our youth, be reminded that its use may decrease motivation and interest in educational and career pursuits that we parents expect and demand from our offspring.

In addition, your son is not living up to the expectations of the family. You, as the parent, have the right to set rules, regulations, standards, goals, and principals for the child to live by. You do not have to accept his edicts that replace common sense, morality, and good judgment. I advise you to make a serious issue of his smoking marijuana in the attempt to extinguish illegal behavior. Approach the issue in the same way you would approach any serious misbehavior.

You may need to look into a drug rehabilitation program to break the bond with the addictive elements of his drug use. If he remains resistive to treatment, consider the possibility of treatment through involuntary commitment procedures or with Children and Youth Services in your state.

21. Does psychiatric treatment help the Uncaring Child?

Psychotherapy and psychotropic medications have not made an impact in treating these individuals, primarily because of their inability to learn from past experience. They repeat unhealthy behavior regardless of where it leads. They continue to blame others for their misfortune. They are unreliable, untruthful, and insincere. Although they may give the appearance of responding positively to therapy, their past unhealthy patterns may reappear.

In working with the *uncaring child*, I find it more useful to work with the parents rather than the child, unless the child is willing to truly work on relevant issues. When I am able to readjust and realign parental thinking and behavior, therapy becomes more useful for the child. When the child begins to experience anxiety because of the parents' intrusion in his life he may be more agreeable to work with a therapist.

22. Do Uncaring Children come from specific socio-economic levels?

No! These kids come from every socioeconomic and environmental background. Apparently, a child's genetic or inherited predisposition has little or nothing to do with their background.

23. Do Uncaring Children come from alcoholic families, and do they have a greater tendency to become alcoholics?

In my clinical experience, I have not seen any evidence that would support this stance. As to these children becoming alcoholics, I don't see any difference in this group turning to alcohol than any other group of children. I haven't found any relationship between alcoholism and the *uncaring child*.

24. Why is it so difficult for these children to stop their behavior?

Not only do these kids have difficulty learning from past experiences, they appear to be addicted to their behaviors. They seem to display much of the compulsive behaviors of the alcoholic, drug addict, sex offender, and compulsive over-eater. They can't stop. They appear to be consumed by an inner force that cannot be penetrated by the outside world. This driving and unyielding energy seems to have a will of its own. Psychologically, the *uncaring child* is an addict. His addiction is to his behavior. His misbehavior is the alcoholic's booze. When confronted by his continued misbehavior, he makes promises never to repeat such behavior, but invariably he does.

25. Do I need to see a therapist for my child's problem behavior, or can I do this on my own?

I would recommend that you first attempt to change your child's misbehavior by learning basic child-rearing techniques. They can be learned by reading many of the self-help books on parenting issues (see references). Also, a parent training group in your school, church, or community may be helpful.

I would recommended seeing a family therapist when the target behavior continues and the anxiety of the family increases. Also, a family therapist should be contacted if your child shows evidence of depression, suicidal thoughts or gestures, or any other sign that may need to be evaluated. The family therapist could evaluate other motivation factors that may be disturbing your child to act in an irrational manner. In any case, it is important to know the entire story of what may be taking place with your child to cause disturbing or disruptive behavior.

26. I have a twenty-two-year-old daughter living at home. After school, she worked a few jobs for short

periods of time. She was always a lazy and poorly motivated student. Although she is not working now, she says she is looking for work. I am reluctant to give her money, but she needs gas to look for work. My husband yells at me for giving her money, and she is the source of many of our arguments. I feel as though I am in the middle, between my husband and my daughter. I think I am doing the right thing, but I am not sure.

This appears to be an issue of poorly defined family roles and expectations. Your daughter expects, and is provided with, essential money, food, and lodging. Her lack of ambition and motivation have been obvious for some time now and has become her acceptable behavioral pattern. As her behavior continues, you and your husband remain in conflict.

I would recommend that you and your husband clarify your own expectations of your daughter's role in the family. Is it okay for her to live off of you without putting anything back? Is it okay for her not to have a job or career? Consider taking a stand on her making choices. You could say to her, "In exchange for gas money, we expect you to contribute to the household, either by paying us a reasonable sum of money or by household duties." When she is not working, you can assign her major household responsibilities to cover her contribution. When she is working, you should expect her to make a financial contribution.

This decreases the possibility of her skirting her responsibility to the family and makes her role much clearer. The conflict between you and your husband should also decrease.

27. *My son has just turned twenty-eight. Since he was nineteen, he has been in and out of prison for possession of drugs, grand theft auto and burglary. He has* *been in conflict with society since he was eight. Whenever he gets into trouble, he is always drunk. Throughout the years, my entire family has been bailing him out of one jam or another. Nothing seems to help. He is ripping us apart.*

Your child appears to be one of these children who has turned his early misbehavior into adult antisocial criminal behavior. These are the type of children who ignore any form of consequence for their misconduct. Even when a most extreme form of consequence (prison) results, these children continue in their destructive behavior, seemingly void of good judgment and remorse.

I believe in the concept of "letting go." This is a state of mind in which you are no longer involved emotionally with the individual who continues to resist and refuses to adjust to normal social standards. This is achieved when you are able to say to your son, "I will no longer support you in any way whatsoever, financially or emotionally, until you gain meaningful employment and stay out of trouble for a period of six months. At that time, I will reevaluate your progress and my relationship towards you."

Of course this is difficult for any parent. The very thought of disconnecting from a loved one is frightful. "A mother is there for her child no matter what," is the motto of mothers throughout this country. So fear of abandoning their offspring makes mothers resist the thought of letting go.

But if you look at the process of letting go more clearly, you will see you are not abandoning your child. You are there for him when he makes the decision to be there for himself. When he chooses behavior that is healthy and discontinues his uncaring, unloving, and destructive conduct, you will then choose whether or not you will be there for him. In this way, both of you have choices to make. Only this time, you are clear, with a specific time frame for evaluating his progress.

I feel it is important to discuss another process that is less desirable and possibly destructive for parents to perform. This is the process of "cutting off." Unlike the process of "letting go," when you have given your child certain choices to consider before having the opportunity to regain your support, "cutting off" is when you no longer provide any choice for your child to come back. It is the final decree to your child when you say, "You are no longer welcome in our home no matter what." Some families have said to their children, "You are dead and no longer exist in our minds."

In my opinion, the process of cutting off leaves the family damaged. The act of cutting off is filled with hate and revenge. There can be little justification for this action, and it may result in irreversible harm for all concerned.

28. *I am a widowed mother of a thirty-six-year old divorced son. He has a three-year-old girl who lives with his former wife. He uses all kinds of drugs and associates with undesirable people. This started when he was in high school. He is constantly calling me or coming over to my house to ask for money. I always attempt to persuade him to seek professional help. His usual reply is, "I don't need any. I'll be all right. Don't worry about me." He is currently working as a cook; however, he rarely holds a job for more than six months. I know he uses the money I give him for drugs, but I feel so guilty when I don't give it to him. Nothing I do seems to work. Is there some advice you can give me to assist my son?*

This is certainly a sad and devastating situation, but not uncommon. You appear to fit the profile of co-dependency. Your continued financial support is your contribution to his illness. Although giving him money eases your guilt some-what, it provides a source of food

Ask The Doctor

for his unending addictive hunger.

The first thing I would advise you to do is to locate an AL-Anon and/or Nar-Anon support group. They are support groups for the families of alcoholics and drug addicts. They will aid and support you in your effort to discourage your son's denial system. At the very least, they will offer you assistance in stopping your behavior that helps maintain your son's use of drugs.

The second thing you need to be aware of is that when you begin to improve your behavior, your son's will probably get worse. He may become agitated, depressed, or anxious, and your usual guilt reaction will be to give into him as you have in the past. But now you will have effective support at your side to assist you.

29. *I am the mother of a four-year-old girl who insists on sleeping in our room. She refuses to sleep in her own room and throws temper tantrums when we return her. My husband and I have no privacy. I must admit I have not dealt with her behavior with any consistency. In fact, my husband reminds me that I have allowed her into our room whenever she wants. This situation is becoming more serious because of her increased demand to sleep with us. We have talked to her about the importance of sleeping in her own room, and we have tried not to give into her demands when she displays temper outbursts. We have tried taking away things as punishment. This problem began with her being a sickly child, and I was worried that she might get worse during the night. I brought her into our room as a means of insuring her safety. What can you suggest to help us in this situation?*

As difficult as this situation appears, it is one of the least difficult behavioral problems to resolve. First, you must purchase a clasp to put outside of your child's door;

or reverse the lock on the door knob. Many parents' are fearful of locking the doors to their children's rooms over concerns of abuse or neglect. Unlike abuse or neglect, however, we will allow our children to have choices. She may choose to behave in a socially acceptable manner or not. Locking her door represents the consequence of her choice to behave in a socially unacceptable manner. Conversely, when she chooses to accept her parents' expectation of her to sleep in her own room, her door remains unlocked. In an abuse or neglect situation, children are rarely given choices that will allow them to relieve their anxiety. For example, let us suppose the parents lock this child's door to prevent her leaving her room. The parents refuse to listen to their child's pleas to be let out. The child is left, in terror, locked in her room, without the choice to change the outcome. This would be reprehensible conduct on the part of the parents.

On the other hand, in the non-abusive situation previously cited, the child is never abused or neglected. In fact, the parents remain on a five-minute vigil throughout the night, if necessary, or for as long as it takes to achieve the desired behavior. They are there to ensure their child's safety as well as reassure her of any fear of abandonment. This is quite different from that of the abusive or neglectful parent.

Second, at bedtime, tell your child that you expect her to stay in her room and not to go to yours. Third, when you put your child to bed, inform her that her door will remain locked as long as she attempts to leave her room to go to yours. Fourth, when she begins to display temper outbursts (which she will), refrain from entering her room for *five minutes*. At that time, enter her room and reassure her of your love. You may pick her up to put her into bed, pat her on the back and tuck her in, but *do not pick her up to comfort her.* You may tell her that you will unlock the door when her outburst subsides and she stays in her own room. Also, don't stay for more than thirty seconds. Lock the clasps or door knob and return to your room. Fifth, when she continues to display further outbursts, do not return to her room for another *five minutes*. At that time, reassure her and leave the room within thirty seconds. Tell her again that you will unlock the door when her outburst subsides and she stays in her room.

This behavior may last for several hours. After the child has exhausted herself, she will usually fall asleep. However, her previous behavior will, almost certainly, reoccur. When it does, repeat the steps.

Earlier, I emphasized the importance of the parents not picking up their child and comforting her when entering her room. This is to ensure that the child's temper outbursts do not produce a pleasurable response. If the parents pick up the child and comfort her when entering the room, the child will get the message that her misbehavior will result in pleasure.

30. *What do you do with a child who throws a temper tantrum or just won't settle down while at a restaurant or at the shopping mall?*

I have seen in restaurants, on many occasions, parents disciplining their child for fooling around, yelling, throwing food, or having a temper outburst. Frustrated and angry at their child's lack of positive response, parents resort to yelling, threatening, or striking the child. Faced with the glares of other patrons and frustrated by their helplessness and inability to cope with their child, the parents either become impotent in dealing with the situation or resort to inappropriate, and sometimes, destructive behavior. Sometimes parents simply don't know alternate methods of managing difficult behavior.

When talking, reasoning, and traditional child-raising techniques fail to produce desired behavior, I suggest measures that are designed to stop the child's misbehavior immediately.

Parents can eliminate the behavior through use of *bathroom intervention*. If you are in a restaurant and your simple requests fail to stop your child's disruptive behavior, quickly remove him from the table or wherever misbehavior is taking place. Usher him to the nearest bathroom and discuss his misconduct. In a calm and firm manner, reassure him of your love and respect for him, but let him know that any further incident will result in removal from wherever the problem is taking place. If he persists in misconduct when you return, take him home for further disciplinary action. This action should be in accordance with the program in Chapter Seven.

I have received much positive feedback from parents who have used Bathroom Intervention. I believe the results are due to the unusual environment in which confrontation takes place. The child's compulsive action is interrupted, leaving him unsettled and more receptive to your request. The child is very much aware of his new surroundings and feels intimidated by the comings and goings of the individuals in the bathroom.

Many parents are reluctant to do bathroom intervention because they see it as possible punishment for all family members. In effect, it is, to some degree. Sometimes, everybody has to "bite the bullet" to get the *uncaring child* to behave.

CONCLUSION

Your *uncaring child,* on the surface, seems simply to lack discipline. The difference is that when parents are taught to understand common behavioral problems and effective techniques, misbehavior of most children generally diminishes. With the *uncaring child* however, misbehavior continues. Parents then experience a plethora of unhealthy feelings leaving them impotent to resolve the parent/child conflict.

To understand *uncaring children*, you must first clarify good/bad parents and good/bad children. This concept is crucial in the work with *uncaring children*. Rescuing is fostering pathological behavior and is commonly attempted by "good" parents to reach these children. However, "bad parents" commonly cause "bad" behavior in most children.

With a comprehensive understanding of the *Uncaring Child Syndrome* and enhanced resources, parents will be able to take charge and finally see positive changes in their children.

Regardless of the child's diagnosis, we must continue to work with expectations of positive growth. *Uncaring children*, in spite of their difficult nature, usually have a chance of improvement. Like antisocial adults, these children may mellow and their *uncaring* behavior might diminish as they grow older. Some of these children have been known to improve as a result of sheer parental tenacity. Parents should not give up; they should remain in charge and continue to provide choices, understanding that the outcomes of these choices remain the sole responsibility of the *uncaring child*.

ABOUT THE AUTHOR

Norman E. Hoffman

Dr. Norman E. Hoffman has a full-time private practice in Ormond Beach, Florida, both as a Licensed Marriage and Family Therapist and as a Mental Health Counselor. He holds both a Ph.D. degree in Psychotherapy and an Ed.D. degree in Human Services. He began his work with the Devereux Foundation in 1963, specializing as a Music Therapist for children. He was then offered a clinical internship at the Menninger Memorial Hospital in Topeka, Kansas. That experience led to his first book, *Hear the Music! A New Approach to Mental Health*. In 1975, Dr. Hoffman's work in the field of organic brain damage led to the publication of *"The Hoffman Test for Organicity"*; and he spent the next 10 years working with adolescents, couples, and families before entering private practice. He is a full clinical member of the American Association for Marriage and Family Therapy and a National Certified Counselor by the National Board for Clinical Counselors.

FOOTNOTES

[1] Freud, 1924; Harlow, 1958; Spitz, 1965

[2] Jersild, 1963, p.312

[3] Ginott, 1965, p. 107 & 108

[4] Samenow, 1984, p. 48

[5] Samenow, 1984, p. xiv

[6] Savitz & Johnson, 1978, p. 16

[7] Dinkmeyer, 1983

[8] Rafferty, 1977

[9] Hoffman, 1982

[10] Meltz, 1994

[11] Cleckley, 1976

[12] Chapman, 1976

[13] Rcid, 1978

[14] Chapman, 1976, pp. 78 - 79

[15] Chapman, 1976, p. 114

[16] Samenow, 1984, pp. 26-39

[17] American Psychiatric Association, 1994, pp. 649-650

[18] The American Psychiatric Association, 1994, p.85

[19] Cleckley 1976

[20] Turecki 1989, pp. 103-104

[21] Weisberg and Greenberg 1988

[22] Weisberg & Green, 1988, p. 9

[23] Harrell, T.H., Honaker, L.M., & Gibson, K.D., 1984

[24] Schjederup-Ebbe, 1992

[25] Maslow, 1936

[26] Diane Fossey, 1979

FOOTNOTES - *Continued*

[27] Jane Goodall, 1986

[28] Kinkead, 1959

[29] Kinkead, 1959

[30] Kinkead, 1959, p. 128

[31] Kinkead, 1959, p.130

[32] Kinkead, 1959, p.130

[33] Kinkead, 1959

[34] Klineman, Butler & Conn, 1980

[35] *Helter Skelter*, Bugliosi, 1974

[36] Bugliosi, 1974, p. 638

[37] Bugliosi, 1974, p. 641

[38] Bugliosi, 1974, p. 655

[39] Lindholm, 1990, p. 40

[40] Ardrey, 1976, p. 91

[41] Ardrey, 1976, p. 205

[42] Abraham Maslow, 1954, 1973

[43] Lindholm, 1990, p. 41

[44] Tarde, 1903: 77

[45] Freud, 1959

[46] Gold, 1986

[47] Gold, 1986

[48] Gold, 1986

[49] Diagnostic and Statistical Manual of Mental Disorders, Fourth Edition (DSM-IV), American Psychiatric Association, 1994, p. 79

[50] American Psychiatric Association, 1994, pp. 83-85

FOOTNOTES - *Continued*

[51] Nancy Reagan, (Bennett, 1986, p. iii)

[52] Bennett, 1986

[53] Bennett, 1986

[54] Chapman, 1976

[55] Carl Rogers, 1951

[56] Perls, Hefferline & Goodman, 1951

[57] Skinner, 1953

[58] Staats & Staats, 1963 & Wolpe 1969

[59] Dinkmeyer, 1976 & Gordon, 1975

[60] Kazdin, 1977 & Franks and Wilson, 1974

[61] Kazdin, 1977

[62] Cohen, Filipczak, & Bis, 1968

[63] Toughlove, 1980

[64] Gordon, 1975

[65] Dinkmeyer, 1976

[66] Raine, 1993

[67] American Psychiatric Association, 1994

REFERENCES

American Psychiatric Association. (1994). <u>Diagnostic and statistical manual of mental disorders. (4th ed.).</u> Washington, DC: Author.

Bennett, W.J. (1986). What Works: Schools without drugs. <u>U.S. Department of Education.</u>

Bugliosi, V. (1974). <u>Helter Skelter.</u> New York: Norton. Chapman, A.H. (1976). <u>Harry Stack Sullivan: His Life and His Work.</u> New York: G. P. Putnam's Sons.

Chapman, A. H. (1976). <u>Textbook of Clinical Psychiatry.</u> (2nd ed.). Philadelphia/Toronto: J. B. Lippincott Co.

Cleckley, H. (1976). <u>The Mask of Sanity.</u> St. Louis: C. V. Mosby Co.

Cohen, H. L., Filipczak, J. A., & Bis, J. S. (1968). CASE project. In J. Shlien (Ed.)., <u>Research in psychotherapy. 3.</u> Washington: American Psychological Association.

Dinkmeyer, D. (1976). <u>Systematic Training for Effective Parenting.</u> Minnesota: American Guidance Service.

Fossey, D. (1979). Development of the Mountain Gorilla. In D. A. Hamburg & E. R. McCown (Eds.), <u>The Great Apes.</u> Menlo Park, CA: Benjamin/Cummings.

Franks, C. F., & Wilson, G. T. (1974). <u>Annual Review of Behavior Therapy Theory & Practice.</u> New York: Brunner/Mazel.

Freud, S. (1923). <u>The Ego and the Id.</u> London: Hogarth Press.

Ginott, H. G. (1965). <u>Between Parent & Child.</u> New York: Avon Books.

Goodall, J. (1986). <u>The Chimpanzees of Gombe: patterns of behavior.</u> Cambridge, Mass & London England: The Belknap Press of Harvard University Press.

Gordon, T. (1975). <u>P.E.T.</u> New York: New American Library.

Harlow, H. F. (1958). The nature of love. <u>American Psychologist. 13.</u> 673-685.

Harrell, T. H., Honaker, L. M., & Gibson, K. D. (1984). <u>Child & Adolescent Diagnostic Screening Inventory.</u> Indialantic, FL: Psychologistics, Inc.

Hoffman, C. L. (1982), January). [Discussion with Cheryl Hoffman].

REFERENCES - *Continued*

Jersild, A. T. (1963). The Psychology of Adolescence. New York/London: MacMillan Co.

Kazdin, A. E. (1977). The Token Economy. New York: Plenum Press.

Kinkead, E. (1959). (1st ed. reprinted 1981). In Every War But One. Westport, Connecticut: Greenwood Press.

Kleindienst, L. (1994, January 1). New year brings new laws. The Orlando Sentinel. pp. A1, A14.

Klineman, G., Butler, S., & Conn, D. (1980). The Cult That Dies: Tragedy of Jim Jones and the Peoples Temple. New York: Putnam.

Meltz, B. (1994, March 25). Children must come first, book tells policymakers. The Miami Herald. pp. 1F-2F.

Maslow, A. H. (1936). A theory of sexual behavior in infra-human primates. J. Genet Psychology. 48. 310-338.

Maslow, A. H. (1960). Some parallels between sexual and dominance behavior of infra-human primates and the fantasies of patients in psychotherapy. Journal of Nervous and Mental Disease. 131. 202-212.

Perls, F. & Hefferline, R. R. & Goodman, P. (1951). Gestalt Therapy. New York: Julian Press.

Rafferty, M. (1977). There Is Such a Thing as a Bad Boy. St. Louis: Globe Democrat.

Raine, A. (1993). The Psychopathology of Crime: Criminal behavior as a clinical disorder. New York: Academic Press, A division of Harcourt Brace.

Reid, W. H. (1978). The Psychopath. New York: Brunner/Mazel.

Rogers, C. R. (1951). Client Centered Therapy. Boston: Houghton Mifflin.

Samenow, S. E. (1984). Inside The Criminal Mind. New York: The New York Times Book Co., Times Books.

Savitz, L. D., & Johnston, N. (1978). Crime in Society. New York: Wiley & Sons.

Rafferty, M. (1977). There Is Such a Thing as a Bad Boy. St. Louis: Globe Democrat.

Raine, A. (1993). The Psychopathology of Crime: Criminal behavior as a clinical disorder. New York: Academic Press, A division of Harcourt Brace.

REFERENCES - *Continued*

Reid, W. H. (1978). The Psychopath. New York: Brunner/Mazel.

Rogers, C. R. (1951). Client Centered Therapy. Boston: Houghton Mifflin.

Samenow, S. E. (1984). Inside The Criminal Mind. New York: The New York Times Book Co., Times Books.

Savitz, L. D., & Johnston, N. (1978). Crime in Society. New York: Wiley & Sons.

Schjelderup-Ebbe, T. (1922). Beitrage zur sozialpsychologie des haushuhns. Z Psychol. 88. 225-252.

Skinner, B. F. (1953). Science and Human Behavior. New York: MacMillan.

Spitz, R. (1965). The First Year of Life. New York: International Universities Press.

Staats, A. W., & Staats. C. K. (1963). Complex Human Behavior. New York: Reinehart & Winston.

Turecki, S. (1989). The Difficult Child. New York: Bantam Books.

Weisburg, L. W., & Greenbery, R. (1991). When Acting Out Isn't Acting. New York: Bantam Books.

Wolpe, J. L. (1969). The Practice of Behavior Therapy. New York: Pergamon Press.

York, P. & York, D. (1980). Toughlove. Sellersville, PA: Community Service Foundation.